D1084931

MODERN WORLD NATIONS

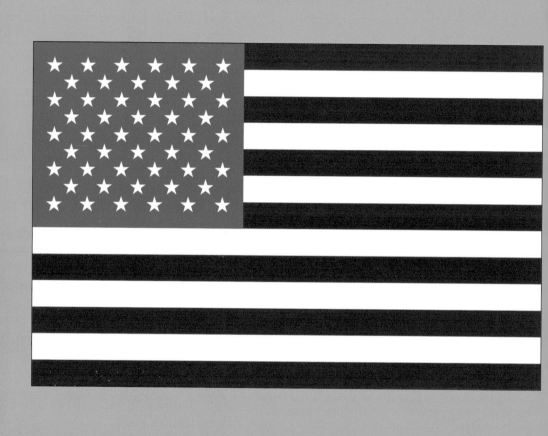

The United States of America

Charles F. Gritzner

South Dakota State University

CHELSEA HOUSE
PUBLISHERS
An imprint of Infobase Publishing

For my grandchildren, Bradley and Jaime Minor and Lucas Swafford

Frontispiece: Flag of the United States of America

Cover: An aerial view of the Washington Monument in Washington, D.C.

The United States of America

Copyright © 2008 by Infobase Publishing

Chelsea House
An imprint of Infobase Publishing
132 West 31st Street
New York NY 10001

Library of Congress Cataloging-in-Publication Data
Gritzner, Charles F.
  The United States / Charles F. Gritzner.
    p. cm.—(Modern world nations)
  Includes bibliographical references and index.
  ISBN-13: 978–0-7910–9511–9 (hardcover)
  ISBN-10: 0–7910–9511–8 (hardcover)
  1. United States—Juvenile literature. I. Title. II. Series.

E156.G75 2007
973—dc22   2007021722

Chelsea House books are available at special discounts when purchased in bulk quantities for businesses, associations, institutions, or sales promotions. Please call our Special Sales Department in New York at (212) 967–8800 or (800) 322–8755.

You can find Chelsea House on the World Wide Web at http://www.chelseahouse.com

Series design by Takeshi Takahashi

Cover design by Jooyoung An

Printed in the United States of America

Bang NMSG 10 9 8 7 6 5 4 3 2 1

This book is printed on acid-free paper.

All links and Web addresses were checked and verified to be correct at the time of publication. Because of the dynamic nature of the Web, some addresses and links may have changed since publication and may no longer be valid.

Table of Contents

The United States of America

1

Introducing the United States

"America the Beautiful . . . From sea to shining sea."

These well-known lyrics, written by Katharine Lee Bates, hold as true today as they did in 1893, when the original verses were penned. On a trip from her Massachusetts home to Colorado Springs, Colorado, Bates was awed by the magnificent view of the Great Plains from atop majestic Pikes Peak. The United States of America truly is a beautiful and bountiful land that has been blessed in countless ways by nature, culture, and history. It is also a country of vast natural and cultural extremes. Through time, the United States has experienced and survived a number of hardships. This brief book attempts to paint a geographical portrait of the land that is home to most readers.

The United States is a land for which superlatives come easily. Its nearly 3.8 million square miles (9,826,630 square kilometers) in

At 3,794,083 square miles (9,826,630 square kilometers), the United States is the world's third-largest country (in terms of land area). It is bordered by Canada to the north, the Atlantic Ocean to the east, Mexico to the south, and the Pacific Ocean to the west.

area rank it third among the world's countries. Only Russia and Canada are larger, but much of their vast lands lie in regions of poorly developed harsh northern climates. The adjoining 48 states lie squarely within the relatively mild and easily developed middle latitudes. With slightly more than 300 million people, the United States also ranks third in population, behind China and India. Unlike in those countries, the American population enjoys one of the world's highest standards of living.

With few exceptions, nature has been kind to the United States. No country can even closely match its environmental diversity. Within its borders can be found all of the world's major climates, ecosystems, and land conditions. This diversity allows the practice of all human activities that are adapted to particular environmental conditions. Similarly, no country can match the United States in terms of environmental extremes, a category in which it holds many world records. The country's unsurpassed economic growth has been bolstered by vast areas of productive land and a wealth of varied metallic, energy, and building resources.

The United States has, however, been ravaged on numerous occasions by devastating natural disasters. In other respects, the country has historically been extremely fortunate. Buffered by two ocean barriers (three if Alaska and the Arctic Ocean are included) and only two neighboring countries, both of which are friendly, the United States has been relatively protected from foreign aggression. Opportunity-seeking European settlers found a sparsely settled land that offered a veritable cornucopia of space, resources, and potential. Within several centuries, following the dream of manifest destiny, Europeans expanded across the continent to the shores of the Pacific Ocean. Unfortunately, this early development was not without a very dark side. It was achieved at the expense of the indigenous Amerindian population, and much of the early economic development in the South was based on African slave labor. This abhorrent practice ultimately contributed to the tragic and bloody Civil War between the North and South.

No country can match America's rich mosaic of human diversity. People from every nation on Earth now call America their home. It has some flaws, but no other country has ever accepted and successfully integrated as many people from more diverse backgrounds than has the United States. The American social and cultural "melting pot" is one of the greatest human achievements in history. Most people who live in the United States—regardless of their racial, national, cultural, ethnic, or other heritage—consider themselves "American." This achievement alone places the United States atop the world's countries in terms of tolerance. The Constitution and the Bill of Rights, a stable democratic government, and a thriving market economy have combined to create an environment in which individuals of all backgrounds can pursue their dreams. Despite a population that passed 300 million in 2006, the country's population density, growth rate, internal migration patterns, and other demographic indices present little cause for concern.

A close relationship exists between a country's government and political stability (or instability) and its economic growth and development (or stagnation). For more than two centuries, the United States has been a model of steadiness in both of these keys to human well-being. Regardless of the political party in power, the government has risen to the occasion when faced with a critical challenge. Of course, there are always critics whose shrill cries of outrage bemoan what they believe is injustice. Nonetheless, such critics are still in this country, and their right to protest without fear of reprisal certainly is one reason why. Economically, the United States is far and away the world's leading power, producing $13 trillion (2006) in annual goods and services. It produces approximately one-fourth of the entire world's economic output. In this capacity, the United States is the economic engine on which much of the world depends for its own economic well-being.

In traveling through the United States, one cannot help but marvel over the seemingly paradoxical similarities and

The New York City metropolitan area is the largest regional economy
in the United States. The city is a center for the arts, finance, insurance,
media, and real estate, and 44 of America's Fortune 500 companies
are headquartered there. Here, commuters make their way into the city
during the morning rush hour.

diversity. Regardless of one's location, certain conditions will be familiar: the language spoken; beliefs in regard to institutions such as government and religion; social expectations and interactions; various corporate chains that offer dining, retail sales, banking, and other services; laws that govern driving, conduct, and other behavior; and much else. Such homogeneity is best appreciated when one can compare and contrast these conditions with those of many other regions. In Europe, for example, during a single day, the author has traveled through areas in which five different native languages were spoken. In Nepal, which is considerably smaller than his home state of South Dakota, more than 120 different languages are spoken! Nonetheless, particularly for someone who has a keen geographic eye, the United States is anything but bland. In fact, if one looks closely, he or she will be treated to a remarkable banquet of varied physical and cultural features and conditions.

The United States of America has been and continues to be an astonishing environmental, human, and cultural experiment on a grand scale unparalleled in history. It is a country that, in many respects, continuously reinvents itself when faced with the need to adapt to changing conditions and new challenges. Currently, a number of troubling conditions are on the horizon; according to some observers, they have the potential to deliver a deluge of change. Many Americans worry about the outcome of the ongoing Middle Eastern conflicts. With two-thirds of the world's total petroleum reserves and current production located there, what would happen to the energy-dependent global economy if the region fell into chaos? Immigration, an aging population, the soaring national debt, energy-related concerns, and environmental changes are among the other issues that deeply concern many Americans.

Before going further, it is important to define several key terms and concepts that appear throughout the book. The term *culture*, as used here, refers to a people's "way of life," how they live—their language, religion, diet, how they make a living, and so forth. The word *society* refers to human groups and interactions. For example, we can refer to "American culture" and "U.S. society." In the first context, the reference is to how Americans live and in the second how they interact with one another. *Race*, or one's *biological inheritance*, refers exclusively to physical (genetically acquired) features. There is no cause-effect relationship what-soever between race and culture. *Races* on the other hand, are arbitrarily determined social creations with little, if any, valid-ity or meaning. People, of course, do differ in appearance, but such differences are minor when compared to those that relate to culture or socioeconomic status.

Other potentially confusing terms relate to the region, country, and U.S. residents. During recent years, it has been increasingly commonplace to refer to the United States and Canada as "North America," rather than as "Anglo America." This distinction recognizes the region's cultural diversity (*Anglo* means "English"), but it is incorrect and confusing. North America is a continent that extends northward from the politi-cal boundary between Colombia and Panama. Therefore, to avoid unnecessary confusion, the author prefers to use *North-ern* America in reference to the cultural region formed by the United States and Canada.

It is also important to understand that the term *America(n)* technically applies to all residents of the Americas. Only the United States, however, adopted the term *America* in its name, the United States of America. Mexico is officially known as the United Mexican States, and the people call themselves "Mexicans." By historical precedent, residents of the United States of America opted for "Americans" (rather than "United Statesians"!).

Nation is a final term that requires clarification. Perhaps because the country's subpolitical units are called "states," Americans have adopted the term *nation* in reference to the country. This is incorrect. The United States is a *state*, the term used in reference to a political unit. The State Department, for example, is the branch of government that is responsible for interacting with other countries. A "nation," on the other hand, is the *territory* occupied by a *nationality* of people, and it may or may not coincide with a politically governed territory. In speaking of aboriginal America, for example, it is correct to refer to the Cherokee, Iroquois, or Navajo nations.

Some people who live within the United States today do not identify themselves as "American." This is typical of some first-generation immigrants, who retain the national identity of their homeland. When a population feels a sense of belonging (nationality) to their country (state), then they may identify themselves by their country name, as is the case in "America" and "Americans."

This book takes you on a journey through the United States. It begins with a tour of the country's physical landscapes and conditions and then travels through the corridors of time, reaching back to the earliest aborigines, the arrival of the Europeans and the resulting clash of cultures, and the evolution of the United States as the major power on the world stage. Subsequent chapters take an in-depth look at the country's population and settlement, government and its role, and economic conditions and development. With this background information, you are ready to tour the country for a glimpse of contemporary life in the United States. Finally, we attempt to see what the future holds for the United States of America and its people.

2

Physical Geography

Nature has blessed and in some ways cursed the United States. No country on Earth can match America's diverse physical conditions and the resulting natural landscapes. The United States holds the distinction of being the only country that has within its territory all of the world's climates and ecosystems (a combination of climate, natural vegetation and animal life, soils, and water features). From the vast and productive "fruited plains" to the "purple mountain majesties" described in Bates's "America the Beautiful," the United States is home to some of the world's largest and most stunning landform features. The country possesses a veritable cornucopia of natural resources. They have been a key factor behind the phenomenal development that has made the United States the world's leading economic powerhouse. Rivers, lakes, and groundwater supplies have provided ample water for domestic, agricultural, and industrial use. The Mississippi River system, the Great Lakes, and multiple outlets

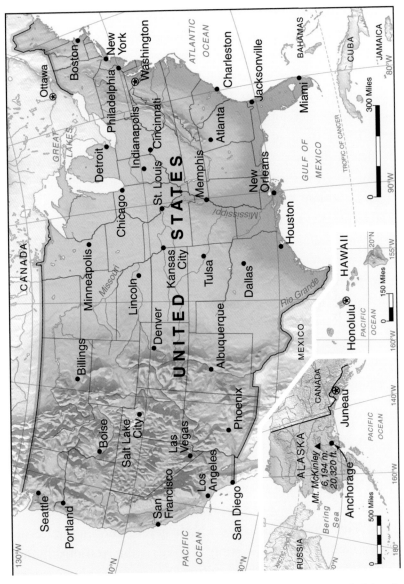

The terrain of the United States is quite diverse. From the coastal plain of the Atlantic Seaboard, the land gradually slopes upward to the Piedmont and Appalachian mountains. From just west of the Appalachians to the Rocky Mountains—a distance of nearly 1,500 miles (2,414 kilometers)—the country is relatively flat. From the Rockies, to the Pacific Coast, the terrain is primarily elevated; although the nation's lowest point, Death Valley, is located in Southern California.

to the global sea give the United States the world's most extensively used navigation network. In terms of its physical geography, the United States truly is a land of superlatives!

A variety of natural environmental conditions afford a country many options for different land uses and kinds of economic development. Crops, for example, are adapted to different types of climate and soil. Because of the environmental diversity in the United States, any crop in the world can be grown somewhere in the country. Even terrain plays an important role. The "amber waves of grain" to which Bates referred depend on vast, relatively flat land holdings that can be farmed with large agricultural equipment. Within the context of a particular culture, certain environmental conditions can be important. Natural harbors located at or near river mouths, for example, are extremely important to a country that is engaged in manufacturing and commerce on a global scale. Mountain scenery, steep slopes, and a deep snowpack are important to people who are affluent and mobile enough to enjoy vacations, skiing, and perhaps even living in a scenic landscape.

Nature presents many challenges, as well as opportunities. The United States is unique in that it is also the only country in the world that is subject to the wrath of *all* natural hazards. Such events—whether geologic, weather related, waterborne, fire related, or the result of some other natural element—can and often do pose a serious threat to life and property.

This chapter focuses on both nature and cultural ecology. Cultural ecology, simply defined, is the relationship that humans—based on their culture (needs, technology, capital resources, economic system, and so forth)—establish with the natural environment(s) in which they live. The study of such relationships is one of the most fundamental geographic themes. Each environment offers a variety of opportunities and challenges, although humans can often add what nature has not provided. Irrigated agriculture, the building of dams and reservoirs and the uses of both, and importing petroleum and other resources serve as examples.

Despite its environmental diversity, the basic way of life practiced by Americans is fairly similar regardless of the location. When thinking about cultural ecology, geographers seek answers to three questions. First, how do people adapt to the environments in which they live? Such patterns often vary greatly from culture to culture and also change through time. Second, what natural elements are important to a people and how are natural resources used? A splendid example of differing perceptions is provided by Alaska's Arctic National Wildlife Refuge (ANWR). Many European Americans value the area's great potential to produce petroleum and natural gas. On the other hand, some native peoples value the caribou herds on which their culture was largely based. Finally, how have humans changed the environments in which they live?

THE LAND AND ITS FEATURES

The United States offers a varied mosaic of landform types—broad plains, rolling hills, rugged plateaus, and majestic mountains. Such diversity offers many opportunities for different types of land use and economic development. Each environment is well suited to some activity, assuming that the culture, technology, and capital resources can support human needs and desires. This reality is reflected in the recent rapid population growth and economic development experienced in areas such as the desert Southwest and the Mountain West. In some areas, such as the Colorado Plateau, aridity and poor soil limit agricultural development, resulting in a very sparse population. However, the region is home to some of the world's most spectacular landform features that result from water erosion: Arizona's Grand Canyon National Park and Utah's Bryce Canyon, Zion, and Arches national parks and Cedar Breaks National Monument. The area's natural wonders attract millions of tourists each year. Our tour of the nation's physiographic areas begins with the Pacific region.

Mountains and Valleys of the Pacific Region

The Pacific region extends from California to Alaska and includes Hawaii. It is home to the country's greatest mountain ranges, its highest (and "tallest") mountains, and some of the continent's most stunning scenery. Here, all three of nature's land-building processes—volcanism, faulting, and folding—are at work. It is also a region in which the agents of erosion—glaciers and swift-flowing streams, in particular—have sculpted spectacular physical landscapes.

Volcanic activity created the Hawaiian Islands; Alaska's Aleutian Islands and many of its mountains; and the Cascades of northern California and western Oregon and Washington. Volcanism is an ongoing process in each of these regions. In fact, the world's most active and extensively studied volcano is in Hawaii (on the big island) in Volcanoes National Park. There, Kilauea Crater "erupts" continuously, although in a gentle, bubbling, non-life-threatening fashion. Two other high peaks on the tropical island of Hawaii occasionally have caps of snow. Hawaii's highest peak, Mauna Kea, rises about 20,000 feet (6,096 meters) from the Pacific floor and reaches an elevation of 13,796 feet (4,205 meters) above sea level. Measured from base to peak, it spans a distance of almost 34,000 feet (10,360 meters), making it the world's "tallest" mountain (though obviously not the highest above sea level).

On the mainland, hills and low mountains form a series of coastal ranges. Many of these features are the result of geologic *folding*, formed by the colliding Pacific and North American tectonic plates. Only in Alaska (in various ranges) and Washington (the Olympic Mountains and National Park) do high mountains hug the coast. Moving inland, uplands give way in several locations to fertile valleys that rank among the country's most productive agricultural areas. They include the

Imperial Valley and Central Valley (formed by the combined San Joaquin and Sacramento valleys) in California, Oregon's Willamette Valley, and the lowlands that border Washington's Puget Sound.

A series of high mountain ranges that are part of the Pacific "Ring of Fire" extend from California northward to Alaska and continue into Asia. This region is a zone of geologic instability that includes all lands bordering the Pacific. As the Pacific and other tectonic plates crunch and grind away, they are responsible for more than 80 percent of the world's seismic (earthquake) and volcanic activity.

The Sierra Nevada, central California's towering "backbone," is an excellent example of an uplifted *fault block* range. From its crest, the forest-covered western slope drops gradually over a distance that averages about 80 miles (130 kilometers). The upward-thrust eastern edge of the range features majestic Mount Whitney, a 14,494-foot (4,418-meter) peak that is the highest point in the adjoining 48 states. The eastern escarpment (slope) of the Sierra offers spectacular scenery as it drops more than 14,000 feet (4,267 meters) in a distance of only several miles. Incredibly, about 60 miles (100 kilometers) east of Mount Whitney, Death Valley plunges to a depth of 282 feet (86 meters) below sea level. This is not only the lowest spot of dry land in the Western Hemisphere, it is the third-lowest point of dry land on Earth!

Many of Alaska's towering, snow-clad mountains also are of fault block origin, including the Alaska Range. Here, buried beneath a mantle of snow and glacial ice, Mount McKinley (also called Denali) is North America's highest peak. No mountain can match McKinley's local relief, thereby making it the world's "tallest" (although not the highest) and one of the most imposing peaks above sea level. From a base near sea level, it soars to an elevation of 20,320 feet (6,194 meters) in a distance of about 20 miles (32 kilometers).

Alaska's Mount McKinley, or Denali, is the highest point in the United States, rising to an elevation of 20,320 feet (6,194 meters). Although its summit is more than 9,000 feet (2,700 meters) lower than Mt. Everest's, Denali is the world's tallest mountain with a vertical rise of 18,000 feet (5,500 meters), compared to 12,000 (3,700 meters) for Everest.

Beginning in northern California and extending northward into Washington are the volcano-formed Cascades. The highest peak is spectacular snowcapped Mount Rainier, which rises 14,410 feet (4,392 meters) above the surrounding lowlands. In 1980, the violent eruption of Washington's Mount St. Helens was a stark reminder that the Cascades remain a very active volcanic range. Alaska has more than 100 volcanoes, many of which are extremely active.

Mountains, Plateaus, and Basins of the Interior West

The western interior offers a variety of huge basins, rugged plateaus, deep canyons, and soaring mountains—all of which contribute to some of the nation's most spectacular terrain. Basin-and-range topography dominates the region between the Sierra Nevada and the Cascades and eastward to the Rocky Mountains and western Texas. Here, relatively low and scattered mountain ranges separate broad and relatively flat basins. Many of the basins have interior drainage, or no outward flow. When water flowing into the basins evaporates, salts are left behind to accumulate. Of the many such areas in the American West, Utah's Bonneville Salt Flats is the best known. Some basins contain large saltwater bodies, such as Utah's Great Salt Lake and southern California's Salton Sea. In most basins, though, lakes do not last. They form after a period of rainfall, only to evaporate quickly and disappear, leaving behind a salty encrustation as evidence of their brief existence.

Two huge plateaus occupy the inland Pacific Northwest and the "Four Corners" area of the Southwest. The Columbia Plateau covers portions of eastern Washington, northeastern Oregon, and western Idaho. It is of volcanic origin, formed by magma and lava that poured across the land millions of years ago and accumulated to a depth of up to 6,000 feet (1,829 meters). In addition to its many volcanic features, the plateau offers several other unique landscapes. About one-sixth of its surface is covered by *loess*, or very fine powderlike material that was deposited by the wind from glacial outwash material during the ice age. This hilly region, the Palouse, contains some of the country's most fertile soil and best wheat-growing land.

The region also has a number of remarkable features scoured by water erosion. Hells Canyon is a yawning 8,000-foot-(2,438-meter-) deep chasm on the Snake River between northeastern Oregon and western Idaho. It is the deepest river gorge in North America, nearly half a mile (one kilometer) deeper than Arizona's Grand Canyon. The Columbia Plateau also is the site of what may be the world's strangest erosional landscape: eastern Washington's "Scablands."

The Scablands are a lunar-like landscape of bare rock. Thousands of years ago, during the late stages of the ice age, a huge lobe of glacial ice dammed today's Clark Fork River near Sandpoint, Idaho. As water built up behind the barrier, it created ancient Lake Missoula, a water body that extended well into western Montana and reached a depth of about 2,000 feet (610 meters). Ice floats, and eventually, the giant lobe began to rise. This caused an immediate breakup of the ice. The result was an event believed by some scientists to have been the world's most destructive flood. A torrent of water with a volume estimated to have been 10 times that of the entire world's river flow was unleashed. Imagine the destruction as the churning water rushed toward the Pacific Ocean at speeds up to 65 miles per hour (105 kilometers per hour)! The force of the raging flood scoured everything in its path, leaving a scablike landscape that is unique to the region.

The Colorado Plateau, composed of alternating layers of sandstone and limestone, is centered on the Southwest's Four Corners area, where the states of Utah, Colorado, New Mexico, and Arizona meet. Water erosion is primarily responsible for the region's towering cliffs, many natural bridges and arches, and deep gorges. Eight national parks in southern Utah alone feature landscapes that were formed by water erosion. In northern Arizona, the Colorado River scoured the spectacular Grand Canyon. This gorge, although not the world's largest, certainly ranks among its best-known and most scenic natural attractions.

The Rocky Mountains extend from northern New Mexico to Montana and as a mountain chain northward into Canada and

Northern Arizona's Grand Canyon is one of the United States' most breathtaking natural sites. The gorge, which is best viewed at sunrise or sunset when its colors are enhanced, was carved by the Colorado River over a period of nearly 2 billion years.

into Alaska. The Rockies actually are a series of mountain ranges, each of which is recognized by a regional name. The highest points in New Mexico, Colorado, Wyoming, Montana, and Idaho are all Rocky Mountain peaks. Colorado alone has 17 peaks that reach an elevation of more than 14,000 feet (4,267 meters). The state's highest peak, 14,433-foot (4,399-meter) Mount Elbert, also is the highest elevation in the American Rockies. Mountain glaciers have scoured the jagged terrain for which the mountains are so famous. Colorado's Rocky Mountain National Park, Grand Teton National Park in Wyoming, and Glacier National Park in Montana all offer marvelous glacier-carved scenery.

Interior Lowlands

Moving eastward from the Rocky Mountains and stretching to the Appalachians is a huge area of lowland plains. The western portion, the Great Plains, lies west of a line that roughly coincides with the 100th meridian and includes portions of Texas, New Mexico, Colorado, Wyoming, North and South Dakota, and Montana. On the western margin (where Denver, Colorado, calls itself the "Mile High City"), they reach an elevation of more than 5,200 feet (1,585 meters). Eastward, the plains drop very gradually in elevation until they reach the Missouri and Mississippi rivers. Generally flat terrain is broken in places by isolated buttes, mesas, and low mountains such as South Dakota's Black Hills, site of America's famous "shrine to democracy," Mount Rushmore. The highest peak in the Black Hills, 7,242-foot (2,207-meter) Harney Peak, is also the highest point in Northern America east of the Rocky Mountains.

East of the Great Plains and extending across the Mississippi River basin to the foothills of the Appalachians is a region variously called the Central or Interior Lowlands or Plains. The area extends from north-central Texas to the eastern Dakotas and eastward to Ohio and Michigan. The region coincides with America's "breadbasket." Excellent soils, ample moisture, and large expanses of flat land that allow the use of heavy equipment help make this region one of the world's most productive agricultural areas.

Appalachian Mountains

The Appalachians are an ancient system of low mountains that extend from Alabama to New England (and into eastern Canada). From the air, they give the appearance of an accordion-like series of parallel, southwest-northeast–trending ridges and valleys. This unique land form is the result of geologic folding. Millions of years ago, forces that worked from within the earth pushed toward one another, creating a ripplelike landscape. The mountains are relatively low, reaching their highest elevation of 6,684 feet (2,037 meters) atop Mount Mitchell in western North Carolina. Initially, the Appalachians formed a divide between the eastern seaboard and the country's interior. As the land was forced upward, however, ancient rivers scoured narrow east-west–trending valleys called "gaps." These passageways, such as the famous Cumberland Gap, located at the point where Kentucky, Tennessee, and Virginia meet, created corridors followed by early Amerindians, European pioneers, and, later, railways and highways.

Piedmont and Atlantic and Gulf Coastal Plains

Immediately to the east of the Appalachians is a hilly upland area that gradually drops toward the coastal plain. Its name comes from its location: *pied* (foot) and *mont* (mountain). At the point where the Piedmont and the coastal plain join is a narrow strip called the "fall zone" or "fall line." The name, of course, comes from falls or rapids that occur along streams that flow eastward from the mountains. These areas became important points for early settlement.

Rapidly flowing water provided an ideal site for water-powered saw, flour, and other industrial mills. It also marked the head of navigation on streams that flowed from the mountains to the Atlantic Ocean. Goods being transported by water had to be placed on land-based vehicles (and vice versa) in a process called "break in bulk." Warehouses often developed around such sites to take advantage of the need for storage. Lively trade and commerce also are associated with such locations. Nearly 30 cities were founded and grew as a result of the many advantages offered by the fall zone (line). They include Philadelphia; Baltimore; Washington, D.C.; Richmond, Virginia; Raleigh, North

Carolina; Columbia, South Carolina; Augusta, Georgia; and Tuscaloosa, Alabama.

A low-lying, flat-to-gently-rolling coastal plain extends from New Jersey to Texas. Regionally, it is divided into the Atlantic and Gulf coastal plains. The Atlantic portion extends from the mouth of New York's Hudson River to eastern Florida. The Gulf coastal plain includes an arc that extends from western Florida to southern Texas. Along the coast, thriving urban centers such as Boston, Massachusetts; New York City; Tampa, Florida; and the Galveston Bay area of Texas all developed as seaports. Ample freshwater, fertile soils, woodlands, and access to the sea combined to make this region attractive to early settlers.

CLIMATES AND ECOSYSTEMS

With the exception of Alaska and Hawaii, the United States lies within the easily developed and environmentally less-challenging temperate midlatitudes. Most of the country experiences relatively moderate conditions of weather and climate. With the exception of aridity, nearly all extremes are seasonal rather than lasting year-round. Even where nature imposes a challenge, such as in the arid West, settlers have found ways to make the land bountiful. Water storage and diversion, irrigation, air-conditioning, insulation, and artificial heating are just some of the ways in which Americans are able to adapt to the extremes that exist.

As mentioned previously, the United States is the only country that includes within its territory each of the world's climates and ecosystems. At the extremes are frigid arctic conditions in northern Alaska, the steaming tropics of Hawaii, and the parched deserts of the Southwest. All other climates occur somewhere within the adjoining 48 states. Varied climatic conditions are important for several reasons. First and foremost, climate is the major control of ecosystems. Because of its many climates, the United States has a tremendous diversity of natural vegetation, animal life, soil conditions, and water features. Also, environmental diversity makes any human activity, including all types of farming, possible someplace within the country. Finally, if there is any truth to the statement "variety is the spice of life," then Americans are indeed fortunate. A marvelous multitude of environments offers unlimited opportunities for development. Geographers identify, name, and classify climates and ecosystems in many ways. In the section that follows, the author uses descriptive terminology to the degree possible.

The Humid East

East of roughly the 100th meridian, the United States experiences a humid climate. In the Southeast, humid subtropical conditions prevail. Moisture is ample: Most locations receive 40 to 60 inches (100 to 150 centimeters) of precipitation per year and some places get considerably more. The Gulf Coast region, southern Florida, and portions of Appalachia receive 60 to 80 inches (150 to 200 centimeters). Severe drought is infrequent. With an annual average 55 inches (140 centimeters) of precipitation, Louisiana is the nation's wettest state as measured by the statewide average of all recording stations. Moisture falls throughout the year, although a peak occurs during the summer months because of convectional thunderstorms. Winters tend to be mild. Freezing temperatures and snow are very rare in Florida and along the Gulf Coast. Temperatures drop and snowfall increases as one moves northward and inland from the moderating influence of the ocean. Summers are long, hot, and sauna-like due to the region's high humidity.

The Northeast experiences a humid continental climate. Ample moisture is received throughout the year, although the total is slightly less than throughout most of the South. Driest conditions occur in the western portion of the region: Much of the Corn Belt receives an average 20 to 40 inches (50 to 100 centimeters) of moisture. Eastward, the amount increases: Coastal and upland areas receive 40 to 60 inches (100 to 150 centimeters) annually. Snowfall is common during winter months and can cover the ground from November through April (or even longer) in some northern areas. Annual amounts in excess of 100 inches (250 centimeters) are not uncommon, particularly in locations that receive "lake effect" snow (winds pick up moisture as they blow across the Great Lakes). Summer temperatures tend to be moderate, but winters can be frigid. Some northern locations have a January temperature *average* that ranges between 0 and 10°F (−12° to −18°C). The region does hold one weather-related record: A weather station atop New Hampshire's Mount Washington experienced a sustained surface wind of 231 miles per hour (372 kilometers per hour), the highest straight wind velocity ever recorded on Earth's surface.

Under natural conditions, the eastern half of the United States supported a dense cover of broadleaf, needleleaf, or mixed forests. Today, much of the natural vegetation cover has been cleared for agriculture and other types of land use. In both climate zones, but particularly in the southeastern United States, a considerable amount of land that was once cleared for agriculture is being returned to woodland. Birds, marine life, and mammals large and small abound in the eastern United States. Conservation programs have actually increased many wildlife populations over what they were a century ago. As the country becomes increasingly urbanized, rural populations decline, thereby actually increasing wildlife habitat. Soils vary greatly in quality from place to place. In the far north, they tend to be thin, acidic, and generally poor. Throughout much of the South, soils were destroyed by poor agricultural practices. Corn Belt soils of the Midwest, however, are among the richest in the world.

The Dry Interior West

Most of the country's western interior—an area that extends from the desert Southwest and eastward from the Sierra Nevada and Cascades to approximately the 100th meridian—receives scant moisture. Both high and low temperature extremes are much greater here than in the eastern part of the country. In this region, actual temperature conditions vary depending on latitude and elevation. Most of the area receives less than 20 inches (50 centimeters) of precipitation annually. The desert Southwest, including much of eastern California, Nevada, portions of Utah, the southern half of Arizona and New Mexico, and western Texas, receives less than 10 inches (25 centimeters) of precipitation per year. Nevada is the nation's driest state, with an annual average of 9 inches (23 centimeters) of precipitation, and Las Vegas is the driest city, receiving about 4 inches (10 centimeters) of moisture each year. The distinction of being the nation's driest spot goes to the parched desert floor of Death Valley, California, which receives a scant annual average of 1.4 inches (3.6 centimeters) of rainfall. Despite its extreme aridity, during the very wet spring of 2005, a large lake formed on the valley's floor! Another record goes to Tucson, Arizona. That city holds the distinction of having recorded the world's lowest relative humidity—a bone-dry 0.8 percent (statistically 1 percent). Summer is the wettest season, when most rain falls in torrential thunderstorms.

The region's aridity is the result of two primary influences. As prevailing winds blow from west to east across the high mountains, most of their moisture is released on the windward (western) side. As they descend down the leeward (downwind) side of the Sierra Nevada and Cascades, they warm, creating a "rain shadow" effect. East of the western mountains, only scattered mountain peaks catch enough moisture to support forest growth. In the desert Southwest, a second control influences aridity. The region is overlain by a semipermanent high pressure system. If you have seen the face of a barometer, you know that rising (higher) pressure is associated with stable weather conditions. This condition persists throughout most of the year in these drier areas of the country.

Because of its continental location or as a result of its being far removed from the moderating influence of the ocean, the interior West commonly experiences weather

Southern California's Death Valley is a land of extremes: It is the nation's lowest point (282 feet, or 86 meters, below sea level) and driest spot (1.4 inches, or 3.6 centimeters, of annual precipitation). Here, the lack of rainfall has caused the ground to crack in Death Valley National Park.

extremes. Summers can be fiercely hot and winters frigidly cold. Temperatures have reached a sizzling 135°F (57°C) in California's Death Valley, only one degree below the world's record high registered in the Sahara Desert. Throughout the region, but particularly in the desert Southwest, afternoon temperatures can soar higher than 100°F (40°C) for weeks on end. Low temperatures are a function of latitude and elevation. Throughout the winter months, the nation's low temperature is often recorded in spots such as Wisdom, Montana; Stanley, Idaho; or even Bellemont, Arizona. Each of these communities is located at a very high elevation. The lowest temperature ever recorded in the 48 coterminous states was a frigid −70°F (−57°C) at Rogers Pass, Montana.

Before the arrival of Europeans, much of the central interior was covered with a seemingly endless sea of grass. From west to east, shorter *steppe* grasslands gradually gave way to taller *prairie* grasses as precipitation amounts increased. This region was home to the American bison (buffalo), an estimated 60 million of which roamed the grassland-covered plains. Within a century, their numbers plummeted to about 1,100 in one of the greatest mass slaughters in history. Other large animals that roam the plains include deer, elk, and antelope. Where water is available for irrigation, soils tend to be quite fertile. Because of the aridity, nutrients have not been leached (washed out).

The Pacific Region

Because it borders the Pacific Ocean, coastal California southward of approximately 40°N latitude experiences a mild and very pleasant Mediterranean climate. In fact, many people believe the Mediterranean to be the world's most pleasant environment. This is one reason why "sunny Southern California" has been a primary magnet for migration for many decades. Summer temperatures rarely reach into the 80s°F (mid-20s°C), and freezing temperatures are unknown in many locations. Severe storms are uncommon. Despite the summer drought and lack of storms, much of the region receives 30 to 50 inches (75 to 125 centimeters) of rainfall annually. Mediterranean weather is unique in one major respect—it is the only climate that experiences summer drought. Weeks can pass during the summer months without a cloud appearing in the sky. Natural vegetation is chaparral scrub and grassland, with many eucalyptus species that were introduced from Australia during the mid-1800s. Native wildlife has largely succumbed to human population growth and destruction of natural habitat.

Coastal northern California and the Alaskan panhandle have a soggy West Coast marine climate that is moist and temperate. Compared to locations at comparable latitudes, the region's summer temperatures are considerably cooler and winter temperatures much warmer. Some locations may go years without experiencing snowfall, something unheard of east of the Cascades. The area that lies west of the mountains is the wettest portion of the continental United States. Warm moisture-bearing winds that blow in from the Pacific are forced aloft over mountains soon after they reach the coast. Rising air cools, condenses, and is ripe for precipitation. Cities such as Seattle, Washington, can go weeks at a time without sunshine. Because of the constant high humidity and frequent drizzle, it is often jokingly said that residents of the region do not die, they just rust away! The wettest spot in the continental United States is in northwestern Washington's Olympic Peninsula, where up to 150 inches (380 centimeters) of moisture falls each year. Several locations in the Cascades and Sierra Nevada receive several hundred inches of snowfall each winter. The snowfall record belongs to Washington's Mount Baker Ski Area. During the winter of 1998–1999, it was buried beneath an incredible 1,140 inches, or 95 feet (2,896 centimeters, or 29 meters), of snow!

This region is home to some of North America's most remarkable forests. Reliable moisture and high relative humidity, including frequent fog, are ideal for tree growth and fire suppression. Until recent years, when the harvest was sharply reduced as a result of environmental issues, the largely needle-leaf evergreen forests of the Pacific Northwest provided most of the country's high-quality lumber. California alone can boast of three enviable world records held by trees growing there. The world's tallest tree is a redwood in an undisclosed (for protection) location in northern California's Redwood

National Park. The towering giant, named Hyperion, reaches a height of 379 feet (115.5 meters). The state also lays claim to the world's largest tree by mass. The General Sherman Tree in Sequoia National Park has a volume of 52,500 cubic feet (1,486.6 cubic meters) and a base diameter of 36.5 feet (11.1 meters). "Methuselah," a nearly 4,800-year-old bristlecone pine located in California's White Mountains, is not only the world's oldest tree, it is believed to be Earth's oldest living thing.

Despite its largely humid tropical climate, Hawaii has an amazing diversity of microclimatic conditions and resulting ecosystems. For a small island, Maui almost certainly holds some kind of environmental record. One can stand in a beautiful Mediterranean-type landscape on the slope of 10,000-foot (3,050-meter) Mount Pu'u' Ula'ula and be within roughly 6 miles (10 kilometers) of nearly all of Earth's ecosystems—from steaming tropical rain forest to water-starved desert and subpolar conditions. Only a polar ice cap condition is missing! An equally amazing extreme exists on the island of Kaua'i. There, one can stand in a desert environment with scant vegetation dominated by grasses, scrub plants, cacti, and irrigated agriculture. Only several miles away, rain falls almost constantly over Mount Waialeale, making it the world's wettest spot with an average 460 inches (168.5 centimeters) of rainfall each year! This anomaly is created by the orographic effect (rain) and rain shadow (aridity).

Much of Alaska experiences short, cool summers and long, often severe winters. Only along the southern coast are temperatures moderate. The capital, Juneau, and largest city, Anchorage, are considerably warmer during the winter months than are many cities in the northern "Lower 48" (as Alaskans refer to the region). Inland, temperatures can plummet to −78°F (−61°C), but also soar to 100°F (40°C). Moisture is adequate throughout the year, although much of it comes in the form of snow that can fall during any month in some locations. Much of the state supports a *taiga* (or boreal) forest composed of dense stands

Located in central California's southern Sierra Nevada, Sequoia National Park is home to some of the oldest and largest trees in the world. The park's Giant Forest contains 5 of the world's 10 largest trees, some of which are more than 250 feet (76 meters) tall, or the size of a 26-story building, and have circumferences of more than 100 feet (30.5 meters).

of larch, pine, spruce, and aspen. Only in the far north does woodland give way to the *tundra*. Here, shallow soils and a very short growing season support a stunted ecosystem dominated by mosses, lichens, clump grasses, and hardy flowering plants. Moose, bears (black, brown, including the huge Kodiak and grizzly, and polar), deer, and caribou thrive here. Marine life includes whales, seals, walrus, and much of the seafood (fish and crab) enjoyed by Americans.

WATER FEATURES

Throughout human history, water has attracted human settlement, economic development, and transportation. Whether Amerindian or European, most early settlements developed around reliable sources of freshwater. The significance of water to human settlement is evident when one studies a detailed political or population map. Observe how many major cities border an ocean, a lake, or a river. This importance also is suggested by the hundreds of towns and cities that incorporate some water feature in their name. How many such communities can you identify that include such terms as *ocean, lake, river, rapid(s), fall(s), spring(s), well, bay, port,* or *harbor?*

Water is essential in many ways. We all know how important it is in our homes when used for domestic purposes. Agriculture, however, is the nation's chief user of water, followed by industry. Shipping by water is the least-expensive means of transportation by a considerable margin. Mills, built at points where streams cascaded over falls or rapids, were an early source of power for milling grain, sawing lumber, and other industrial uses. Today, their importance has been replaced by huge hydroelectricity-producing dams. Both oceanic and freshwater fishing is an important commercial and recreational activity; people flock by the millions to water for recreational purposes. Along coasts, many of the largest cities grew around a river mouth or natural harbor. In the nation's arid interior, nearly all cities are located at oasis sites.

For many Americans, visiting the ocean is a favorite summer pastime. Each year, millions of American vacationers head to such popular destinations as Daytona Beach, Florida, which bills itself as the "World's Most Famous Beach."

Water, one can argue, is the resource most essential to life, yet water-related problems loom on the horizon. A growing population, particularly in the water-deficient Southwest, has pushed available water supplies to their limit. Water pollution is a problem in many areas, including the Great Lakes, many smaller water bodies, and rivers in most areas of the country. Groundwater stores are being polluted in some areas and critically depleted in others.

Oceans

The United States is the only country bordered by three of the world's oceans—the Pacific, the Atlantic, and the Arctic. (Technically, Russia faces on the Baltic Sea, not the Atlantic Ocean.)

This gives the country a tremendous advantage in many ways. Politically, oceans do not "belong" to anyone; hence, they serve as a buffer against potentially hostile neighbors. Economically, they are the source of countless marine resources, scenic beauty (resulting in increased property values), and shipping access to much of the world. Physically, oceans moderate temperatures and serve as the source of atmospheric moisture. With possible continued warming of Earth's atmosphere, the Arctic Ocean may become a major focal point of global navigation. In the absence of thick sea ice, ships could easily pass between Europe, Asia, and North America.

Lakes

An estimated 90 percent of the world's natural lakes were formed by glacial action. During the Pleistocene (ice age), glaciers reached into the United States as far south as the Ohio and Missouri rivers and also formed in many of the higher mountain ranges. Most lakes, therefore, are in the northeastern section of the country and north of the Ohio and Missouri rivers. Elsewhere, in the Southeast and the West, most "lakes" are actually reservoirs, water bodies formed behind dams.

The Great Lakes form the world's largest system of freshwater. In fact, Lake Superior is the world's largest freshwater lake by surface area. Water from the Great Lakes reaches the Atlantic Ocean through Canada's St. Lawrence River. For a half century, ships have been able to pass between the Great Lakes and the Atlantic by way of the St. Lawrence Seaway.

Rivers

The major river system in the United States is that formed by the Mississippi and its two major tributaries, the Ohio and Missouri rivers. This giant network drains about 41 percent of the 48-state area, including all or part of 31 states (and two Canadian provinces). The combined Missouri-Mississippi River is about 3,700 miles (5,970 kilometers) long, a distance surpassed only by the Nile and Amazon rivers. Barges can navigate the rivers upstream to Minneapolis-St. Paul, Minnesota; Pittsburgh, Pennsylvania; and Sioux City, Iowa. New Orleans, Louisiana, located near the mouth of the Mississippi, was one of the nation's leading seaports before Hurricane Katrina's devastating blow in 2005.

Dependence on a river is illustrated by current problems along the Missouri. Severe drought during the first decade of the twenty-first century has caused the river's flow to reach a critically low level. Recreational use, hydroelectric energy production, barge traffic, and even the domestic water supply of some riverside communities have been severely affected as a result.

Many eastern rivers are of local importance. Certainly the Hudson River has played a very significant role in the growth of New York City. In the Southeast, the Tennessee, Cumberland, and other rivers were transformed by one of the world's most massive reclamation projects. Beginning in 1933, during the Great Depression, the Tennessee Valley Authority (TVA) built nearly 50 dams on this drainage system. Their construction spurred the regional economy by creating jobs for tens of thousands of people in one of the nation's poorest regions. The dams also gave the area a clean and inexpensive source of (hydroelectric) energy, controlled flooding that had long plagued the region, and created reservoirs that provide many recreational opportunities.

In the Southwest, the Rio Grande and Colorado River flow southward across desert landscapes. Both streams are of far greater importance than their relatively small volume of water might suggest. In fact, millions of people, huge cities, and billions of dollars in agricultural production depend on their flow. The Rio Grande flows from the Colorado Rockies, through central New Mexico, and into Texas, where it forms the border between the United States and Mexico. It is dammed in three locations, is vital to regional agriculture, and is often dry along much of its lower course.

The Colorado River is controlled by eight dams and reservoirs, including Glen Canyon Dam and Lake Powell on the Utah-Arizona border and Hoover Dam and Lake Mead just east of Las Vegas, Nevada. Huge water diversion projects have artificially supported the Southwest's booming population and economic growth. Phoenix and Tucson, Arizona, draw water from the Colorado River, as do California's Los Angeles basin, San Diego, and the agriculturally productive Imperial Valley. Las Vegas, the nation's fastest-growing city, also depends on the Colorado for its water supply. Coastal southern California also obtains water from streams that flow from the Sierra Nevada. With 35 million residents in California and booming populations in Arizona, Nevada, and the upper basin of the Colorado River, many observers wonder how long it will be before the region faces a severe water crisis. Without the current massive diversion of water, the region could support only a small fraction of its present population. What might happen, for example, if the severe drought that has plagued much of the region since 2000 continues and intensifies?

In the Pacific Northwest, the mighty Columbia and its chief tributary, the Snake River, produce huge amounts of hydroelectric energy. They are also the source of water for irrigation and domestic use and for important recreational resources. Alaska's Yukon River is a large stream but is of little economic significance.

Groundwater

Groundwater is water deposits stored in an aquifer, the upper limit of which is the water table. In arid regions, an aquifer may be nonexistent or may lie more than 1,000 feet (300 meters) below the surface, as is the case throughout much of the desert Southwest. Groundwater is tapped by wells, although in some places it reaches the surface through springs. Throughout much of the country, both the quality and the quantity of groundwater deposits are in sharp decline. Aquifers can easily be contaminated by the seepage of pollutants. Fortunately, monitoring systems can determine when they reach a dangerous level. In many areas, groundwater—some of which is many thousands of years old—has taken on a foul taste or odor because of the earthen material in which it is embedded. Salt and sulfur, for example, can reduce water quality.

In many locations, water from aquifers is being used faster than it is being replaced. This is occurring in the vicinity of many cities in the West. In the country's midsection, from South Dakota to the Texas panhandle, much of the agriculture depends on irrigation with water taken from the Ogallala Aquifer. This aquifer is being mined at a rate much greater than its recharge. The future of this region depends on either finding an alternative source of water or on developing an economy that is in balance with available water resources.

ENVIRONMENTAL HAZARDS

Although blessed in many ways by its environmental diversity, the United States is also unique in an unfortunate way: It experiences a greater variety of natural hazards than does any other country and by a wide margin. Earth's atmosphere, lithosphere, hydrosphere, and biosphere all wreak havoc on land and property and often take a toll on human life. Are natural forces always "at fault"? In this context, we must recognize the difference between a natural *hazard*, something that poses a risk, and a natural *disaster*, a natural occurrence that inflicts damage on human life or property. Simply stated, people who live in hazard-prone areas elect to do so *knowing* that they face potential risk. They bet that nature's wrath will not affect them.

Some places are much safer or much more dangerous than others. In July 1998, the National Geographic Society published a map entitled *Natural Hazards of North America*, which shows the distribution of 11 environmental hazards. Amazingly, a very close correlation exists between population concentrations and both environmental hazards and natural disasters! The most dangerous areas are the Pacific Coast states and the eastern half of the country. Yet these areas are precisely where the great majority of Americans live. Coastal regions, wooded areas, lakeshores, river valleys, and mountains present pleasing visual landscapes to which people flock, making property values soar. In fact, research has shown that the greater the potential environmental risk, the higher the population density and value of property! Ironically, the nation's safest areas—the Great Plains and much of the Great Basin—have the lowest population density, the highest out-migration, and the lowest property values.

The following list presents the nation's 10 worst natural disasters in terms of loss of life. In all instances, figures are estimates, some of which vary greatly:

Year	Disaster	Deaths
1900	Hurricane (Galveston, Texas)	6,000–12,000
1928	Hurricane (Florida Atlantic Coast)	2,500
1871	Forest fire (Peshtigo, Wisconsin)	1,200–2,500
1889	Flood (Johnstown, Pennsylvania)	2,210
1893	Hurricane (coastal Louisiana)	2,000
2005	Hurricane (New Orleans and Louisiana and Mississippi coasts)	2,000
1893	Hurricane (Sea Islands of South Carolina and Georgia)	1,500
1906	Earthquake (San Francisco, California)	500–3,000
1925	Tornadoes (Midwest)	727
1938	Hurricane (New England)	720

Such figures are quite alarming, but to put them in perspective, the total of the above list is 29,000 deaths. On the other hand, *each year* the country experiences about 44,000 highway fatalities, 50,000 violent deaths (murder, suicide, etc.),

Hurricane Katrina ranks among the top 10 most devastating natural disasters in U.S. history. The Category 3 hurricane slammed into the Louisiana and Mississippi Gulf Coast on August 29, 2005, and caused more than $81 billion worth of damage. Here, rescue workers search for survivors a week after Katrina hit New Orleans.

and about 445,000 deaths related to smoking. In addition, it is significant to note that only one of the events has occurred since 1928. Two factors have contributed to the sharp reduction in loss of life. First, forecasting has greatly improved: People can be alerted to many impending events well in advance, thereby allowing them to take necessary precautions. This is particularly true of weather-related hazards such as hurricanes, tornadoes, blizzards, or floods that cause rain or snowmelt. Once generated, tsunamis (incorrectly called "tidal waves") also can be forecast. Scientists are even showing some progress in their attempts to predict earthquakes and volcanic eruptions. A second factor involves engineering and site selection. Today, settlements and structures are much more apt to be located and built with safety in mind. Many other steps can be taken. Dams, levees, preservation of wetlands, and reforestation all reduce the threat of flooding. Cellars offer protection from tornadoes, and improved forest and grassland firefighting strategies and technology can reduce losses from such conflagrations.

Atmospheric hazards include hurricanes, tornadoes, heavy flood-causing rain, blizzards, ice-related storms including hail and sleet, lightning, and drought. Hurricanes, responsible for 6 of the country's top 10 natural disasters, are generally limited to the Gulf and Atlantic coastal zones. Although their winds can be destructive, the greatest damage is caused by water. Along coasts, storm-pushed surges of water up to 20 feet (6 meters) high can rush ashore, destroying everything in their path. Inland, torrential rains can cause severe flooding. In New Orleans, Hurricane Katrina breached protective levees in several places and dropped up to 15 inches (38 centimeters) of rain. It was the nation's greatest urban disaster since the San Francisco Earthquake of 1906. With damage estimated in excess of $80 billion, it also was the country's most costly natural disaster by a wide margin. Tornadoes, blizzards, hail and ice storms, and flooding are commonplace throughout most of the eastern half of the country. Blizzards, drought, and local flooding pose threats in the Great Plains and much of the interior West.

The Pacific Coast is the most hazard-prone area of the United States. It lies within the Pacific "Ring (or Rim) of Fire," a zone of geologic instability that encompasses most of Earth's seismic and volcanic activity. From southern California to Alaska's Aleutian Islands, the Pacific and North American plates slide, crunch, and grind against one another, creating one of

Earth's most earthquake-prone zones. Anchorage, Seattle, San Francisco, and Los Angeles all sprawl across active geologic faults and thus are in constant peril. Volcanoes dot the landscape from the Cascades northward into Alaska and, of course, in Hawaii. Many are active. In 1980, Washington's Mount St. Helens erupted violently. The blast devastated the surrounding area for many miles and caused 57 deaths. Geologists had anticipated the explosion, and the peak is quite isolated, factors that contributed to minimal property destruction and loss of human life. In addition, the Pacific Coast is subject to earth creep and landslides, raging wildfires, and periodic droughts.

3

The United States Through Time

A merican historical geography offers an amazing trip through the corridors of time. It is a journey replete with mystery, adventure, and incredible good fortune. It also chronicles occasional obstacles, detours, and hardships. This chapter investigates the country's past. Geographer Erhard Rostlund once observed that "the present is the fruit of the past and contains the seeds of the future." Just as an adult person is a composite of family genetic material, parenting, education, peer group influences, and so forth, a country is a product of past influences and events.

THE FIRST AMERICANS

Many questions remain unanswered in regard to the first Americans. About all that is known for certain is that they came from elsewhere and are primarily of Asiatic (Mongoloid) physical stock. For seven decades, archaeologists (scientists who study early peoples) believed that the Americas were settled by Asians whose pursuit of big-game animals drew them to this vast unsettled land. Supposedly, they wandered across *Beringia*, the Bering Strait "land bridge" that linked Siberia and present-day Alaska. This corridor was exposed by the drop in global sea level during the ice age. (Because so much ocean water was locked up on land in the form of glacial ice, sea level dropped an estimated 400 feet, or 122 meters.) On entering North America, these people supposedly passed through an ice-free corridor that formed between two huge masses of glacial ice. Finally, they reached the area of Clovis, New Mexico, where their unique projectile points, which date back about 13,000 years, were found.

Today, however, the origin of the first Americans has become one of the most intriguing mysteries that face social scientists. A few scholars have long questioned whether early peoples could have withstood the extremely cold conditions of Beringia and a narrow passageway between two towering masses of glacial ice. Rather than representing a single biological stock, *Amerindians* (American Indians) appear to be a rather diverse group. This suggests the possibility of multiple migrations into the Americas, perhaps involving different routes at different times. A growing number of scientists now believe that the earliest arrivals may have followed a coastal route. They could have walked along the broad continental shelf that was exposed by the lower sea level, perhaps rafting around barriers such as river mouths or glaciers flowing into the sea. Even the time of their arrival is now in doubt. Some hotly contested evidence from South America suggests that humans may have occupied the area most distant from Beringia more than 30,000 years ago! It seems probable that what is now the United States has been home to humans for perhaps 15,000 to 20,000 years.

EARLY NATIVE CULTURES

Native people of the United States recognize themselves by many names. *Indian* is a misnomer. First, the term comes from one of history's great geographical blunders: Columbus's belief that he had reached Southeast Asia's "East Indies." Second, not all native peoples are of Indian heritage. In Alaska, there are Inuit (Eskimo) and Aleut peoples, as well as Athabascan and other native groups. Many Hawaiians are of Polynesian ancestry. Finally, many native peoples prefer to be called First Americans, Native Americans, First Nations, Amerindians, indigenous peoples, or some other more sensitive designation.

Unlike the lingering mysteries surrounding the arrival of the earliest residents of the United States, a number of things are quite well established in regard to them. There is no doubt, for example, that when Europeans "discovered" the "New World," they reached a land that already had been settled thousands of years earlier. Further, most native peoples showed physical features that tied them to a geographic origin somewhere in East Asia. The aboriginal population at the time of European contact remains in doubt. Estimates range widely, but it is probable that they numbered about 2 to 3 million. What is known is that soon after Europeans arrived, warfare and European diseases (against which native peoples had no natural immunity) decimated native populations. Finally, it was a very diverse population. Native cultures varied greatly from place to place, as did their levels of cultural attainment. In the United States alone, native peoples spoke as many as 200 different languages in 17 different linguistic families. This fact suggests multiple origins and migrations, perhaps spread out over a span of many millennia.

Originally, all early peoples practiced a hunting-gathering (and, in some areas, fishing) subsistence economy. Populations were small, material possessions were meager, and most groups moved frequently in search of a more bountiful environment. Perhaps 3,000 to 4,000 years ago, the idea of farming, along with crops such as maize (corn), several types of beans, and squash (including the pumpkin), spread northward from Mexico. This allowed some peoples in the desert Southwest to settle in one place, near a stream or spring, and to grow crops using irrigation. They included the Pueblo people, who built massive

During the twelfth and thirteenth centuries, Pueblo Indians lived in Mesa Verde, cliff dwellings that are located in southwestern Colorado. By the time Spanish explorers came across Mesa Verde in the 1760s, the original inhabitants had long since disappeared.

adobe structures, many of which remain today as reminders of these advanced early cultures.

The idea of farming, along with the crops, gradually spread to more humid lands in the eastern United States. Here, woodland peoples added crop raising to hunting of game animals and birds and fishing the region's lakes and streams. A large and reliable food supply supported remarkable cultural growth that is well documented by early European accounts of the people. Groups such as the Iroquois in the Northeast and Cherokee in the Southeast had large populations, lived in settled communities, and had high levels of social organization and cultural attainment that are associated with high civilizations.

Many cultures that lived near the Pacific or Arctic Ocean depended largely on marine resources for their food supply. They were skilled boatbuilders and fishermen. Watercraft varied from dugout canoes to kayaks and outriggers. Some people, such as native tribes in the Pacific Northwest, depended on salmon taken from the Columbia and other rivers. Fishing techniques varied greatly, as did the means of preserving the catch. Whether in Hawaii, an Alaskan Arctic village, or the Pacific Northwest, though, each tribe had developed a successful strategy for providing an adequate supply of marine resources.

In the country's interior, millions of American bison ("buffalo") roamed the vast plains, where they grazed on the steppe and prairie grasses. Here, 20 different tribal groups became skilled hunters who depended on these huge animals for much of their material culture. From the bison, they obtained food, clothing (hides and sinew used as thread), material for housing, and many of their tools and weapons (bone and horn). Settlement was temporary and material possessions were few, often little more than tools, weapons, and clothing. To avoid overgrazing, bison migrated constantly; hence, the Plains Indians followed a seasonal round as they pursued the herds.

The lowest populations and most meager level of material and nonmaterial culture occurred in a region that roughly coincides with the Great Basin and most of present-day California. Here, wandering tribes depended largely on seed gathering, hunting, and, in some locations, fishing.

Special mention must be made of two amazing cultures—the Inuit (Eskimo) of Alaska and the Polynesians of Hawaii. The Inuit thrived in one of the world's harshest environments. They developed a level of material culture that was one of the most advanced among the world's Mesolithic (preagricultural) peoples. Their houses—variously made of wooden frame, sod, animal skins, and, of course, snow (the well-known igloo)—were warm and sturdy. As hunters and fishermen, they were exceptionally skilled. The Inuit harpoon has been called the most effective hunting tool ever developed by a traditional culture. Their small *kayak* watercraft were so well designed that they are in popular use today far beyond their arctic home. During the frigid winter months, dogsleds provided the means of transportation. This tradition continues today in Alaska's famous Iditarod race. Finally, their clothing (body, headgear, footwear, and gloves) is so well designed that it became the model for modern cold-weather gear. In the Pacific, Polynesian peoples—voyaging more than 2,000 years before Magellan and other Europeans—sailed throughout most of the Pacific Basin in small but sturdy outrigger craft. By the dawn of the Christian era, they had discovered and settled most if not all inhabitable islands in the vast Pacific.

Through time, as European settlement and other influences spread, so did the negative impact of European diseases and other elements that severely disrupted (and often terminated) Amerindian populations and their cultures. In some areas, native populations were completely destroyed. Nearly everywhere, their land was taken, often forcefully, and in many instances they were removed to distant and strange locations. The destruction of Amerindian peoples and their culture is one of the saddest chapters in American history.

EUROPEANS ARRIVE

Little is known about the first Europeans to set foot on what is now the United States. Could it have been Vikings from Scandinavia, as some historical geographers believe? Perhaps an Irish monk? Or possibly Portuguese or Spanish fishermen blown off course who sailed to the rich fishing grounds of Newfoundland's Grand Banks? These are just some of the groups that may have reached American shores well before the first documented landings. What is known is that, in 1492, Christopher Columbus reached a land that he believed to be the spice-rich East Indies. His discovery sparked what became a several-century search for an all-water route through or around the Americas to the Pacific Ocean and the distant riches of Asia.

The first known European to reach the shores of the United States may have been Giovanni Caboto (known in English as John Cabot). Although this is questioned by many, some scholars believe that he reached the coast of Maine in 1497. (Seven years would pass before Columbus made landfall on the continental landmass in 1504.) In 1524, the king of France sent Italian explorer Giovanni da Verrazzano on a voyage to the New World in search of wealth and a route to Asia. Verrazzano reached the coast of present-day North Carolina and continued northward. He is believed to have been the first European to follow the coast of present-day New England. His epic voyage is memorialized by the spectacular Verrazano-Narrows Bridge that spans the mouth of the Hudson River in New York City. Surprisingly, the lure of finding a water route to Asia was so strong that more than a century passed before northwest Europeans began to settle the newly found land! Not until 1607 did the first north Europeans—the British at Jamestown, Virginia—begin to permanently settle the land.

American history often carries a strong north European bias. In reality, much of what is now the United States was first explored, claimed, and settled by Spaniards. In 1540, for example, long before the English or French penetrated the country's interior, Spanish explorer Francisco Coronado explored much of the southwestern United States. In his search for the fabled Seven Cities of Gold, his men explored an area that extended from Arizona eastward into Kansas. In 1565, 42 years before the Jamestown settlement was established, a Spanish foothold was built at St. Augustine (Florida). In the Southwest, the Spanish established a regional capital in Santa Fe (New Mexico) in 1610, a full decade before the Pilgrims settled at Plymouth, Massachusetts.

EUROPEAN ROOTS IN AMERICAN SOIL

Early European settlement in what is now the United States shows distinct regional differences in political and cultural dominance. These patterns resulted from the various economic (and, of course, political) emphases placed on the land and resources by the different European colonists. North Europeans first settled along the mid-Atlantic and New England coasts. There, they harvested timber (which was very scarce in Europe), fished, and cleared land on which to settle and farm. Cities such as Boston, New York, and Philadelphia were established around protected harbors. They served as a doorway for trade between the new settlements and the homelands that lay across the Atlantic.

Inland, throughout the Great Lakes region and Mississippi Valley westward to the Rockies, French trappers pursued valuable fur-bearing animals, particularly beavers. Spaniards lay claim to an area that extended from Florida westward to the Pacific Coast and included much of the interior West. They sought to protect their Caribbean and Atlantic trade routes, expand their territory northward, discover gold, and convert native peoples to the Roman Catholic faith. The cultural influence of these early settlers is still evident in many Spanish, British, French, and other European language place names that dot the American landscape.

By the eighteenth century, the United States was on the brink of history's greatest mass migration. During the next 250 years, 45 million Europeans migrated to America. They came for many reasons: Land was plentiful, and they were free to practice their religious, social, political, and other cultural beliefs without oppression. Many simply wanted to "reinvent" themselves in a new land that offered many attractive opportunities. Others, sadly, came unwillingly as slaves.

Through the process of *relocation diffusion*, each group arrived with its own cultural baggage—language, customs, religion, diet, and other well-established ways of living. Europe is a region of great cultural diversity and a long history of ethnic conflicts. Given this historical reality, what occurred in America borders on a miracle—one unparalleled in all of history. Within a span of several generations, most ethnic ties to the homeland vanished. British, Dutch, Germans, Scandinavians, French, and many others simply blended into a cultural "melting pot" to become "Americans." By the mid-1700s, all lands between the Atlantic Coast and the Appalachians were under British control. A short quarter-century later, despite their varied ethnic backgrounds, the 13 original colonies would free themselves from British political domination. On July 4, 1776, a new country was born: the United States of America.

SOUTHWARD EXPANSION

Regardless of their place of origin, Europeans came from temperate midlatitude lands in which subtropical crops could not be grown. The American South, in contrast, offered a humid subtropical climate with ample year-round moisture and a long, hot growing season. Conditions were ideal for the growing of plantation crops such as cotton, indigo, tobacco, and rice. During the eighteenth century, a plantation-based economy boomed in the South.

Northwestern Europeans (primarily from the British Isles) were unaccustomed to sweltering heat and humidity. As a result, they were unable (or unwilling) to perform hard physical labor on the plantations. At first, they turned to Amerindians as a labor source. From the very beginning of settlement, however, some Europeans had brought African

During the eighteenth century, a plantation-based economy developed in the South that was driven by slave labor. By the eve of the Civil War in 1860, there were more than 3.5 million slaves in the South who primarily picked cotton and tobacco.

slaves to America. The Africans were well adapted to working in hot, humid weather conditions and proved to be excellent laborers in the plantation fields. Sadly, for more than 150 years, the Southern plantation economy depended on and thrived because of African slave labor. Ultimately, slavery was a key issue in the bloody conflict between the Northern and Southern states—a war that sharply divided the country and took 600,000 to 700,000 lives. In the United States, the slave trade was outlawed in 1808, although the practice itself continued until 1865. An estimated 400,000 Africans were unwillingly brought to British Colonial America. Certainly the institution of slavery and the devastating war to which it contributed ranks as the lowest point in U.S. history.

WESTWARD EXPANSION

By the early 1800s, what had begun as a mere trickle of movement westward from the Atlantic coastal plain became a surging flood of humanity following in the footsteps of Daniel Boone and other hardy early pioneers. Like grains of sand passing through an hourglass, land-hungry frontiersmen from the eastern seaboard flowed toward narrow water gaps (east-west valleys cut through mountain ridges) and spilled across the Appalachians into the Ohio Valley and beyond. Hundreds of thousands of people sought a new life and opportunity in the fertile lands that lay in the interior valleys and plains located west of the mountains. Many Europeans, particularly those of Scandinavian and German ancestry, were skilled woodsmen. They knew how to clear land, remove stumps, and build sturdy log homes, fences, and outbuildings. Gradually, following the Ohio River, the Great Lakes, and other routes of easy access, they continued westward. In their wake, canals and railroads followed. These transportation linkages helped to maintain ties between the expanding western frontier and the rapidly expanding population and economic development along the East Coast.

During the mid-nineteenth century, two nearly simultaneous events served as magnets to draw fortune seekers across the country's rugged interior to the West Coast. On January 24, 1848, James Marshall discovered gold at Sutter's Mill, located on the American River near present-day Coloma, a small community at the western foot of the Sierra Nevada in present-day central California. His discovery started a rush that ultimately brought tens of thousands of gold-hungry prospectors (and others)—the "49ers"—to the "Golden State."

With the populations and economies of San Francisco, Sacramento, and nearby areas booming as a result of the gold rush, the need for safe and speedy transportation links with the East became apparent. At the time, several dangerous and time-consuming options for making the journey between the coasts existed. One could travel by water around the tip of South America, a voyage of 15,000 miles that took four to eight months. Many people, however, preferred to sail to Panama, cross the narrow isthmus by land, and then catch another ship to California. This route was 7,000 miles and took up to three months. The tropical land crossing also exposed travelers to malaria and yellow fever. Finally, one could cross the continent by land, an often-treacherous 2,500-to-3,000-mile trek by wagon that could take up to seven months. Shorter trips west of the Missouri River—in those limited areas where service was available—were made by horseback, stagecoach, or riverboat (along the Missouri and several of its larger tributaries).

Clearly, something had to be done. By midcentury, a fairly extensive network of railroads existed in the eastern United States, but none extended far beyond the Missouri River. That, however, was about to change. In 1862, Congress passed the Pacific Railway Act, which authorized the Union Pacific Railroad to begin building westward from Omaha, Nebraska, and the Central Pacific Railroad to start building eastward from Sacramento, California. Nearly seven years later, on May 10, 1869, the tracks joined at Promontory Summit, in present-day Utah, and a golden spike was driven to commemorate the occasion. Later that year, the rails were extended from Sacramento westward to San Francisco, thereby spanning the continent.

After the end of the Civil War in 1865, the United States entered a period of growth and prosperity: Most of the country was linked by both transportation and communication (telegraph) networks. The Industrial Revolution, which had begun in Great Britain a century earlier, was now fully established in the eastern United States. Both the population and the economy were booming, as industries, businesses, and agriculture thrived. Millions of immigrants, most of whom came from Europe, swelled the population and contributed to economic growth. As the country faced the dawn of the twentieth century, it did so with great optimism. America was

In May 1869, the Union Pacific and Central Pacific railroads met at Promontory Summit, in present-day Utah, marking the completion of the Transcontinental Railroad. During construction, both lines had to traverse mountainous terrain, which greatly slowed the railroad's progress. Pictured here is a snowplow that was used to clear the Central Pacific's snow-covered tracks in the Sierra Nevada.

coming into its own as an emerging global power, and the country as a whole was prospering. Storm clouds were forming on the horizon, however.

DECADES OF TURBULENCE

The first half of the twentieth century was an era of turbulence for the United States. Racial and ethnic discrimination were widespread. Between 1914 and 1918, much of Europe was engaged in World War I, a conflict that the United States entered in 1917. U.S. troops played a very significant role in bringing the war to an end in 1918, but not before the country lost an estimated 110,000 to 120,000 service personnel. Soon after the war was over, in 1919, Congress passed the Volstead Act (Prohibition), which prohibited the manufacture, distribution, sale, or consumption of alcoholic beverages. By the time the act was repealed in 1933, organized crime had gained a strong foothold in the country, providing "bootleg" liquor and engaging in other illegal activities.

During the 1930s, the United States reached what many believe to have been its all-time low point. On October 24, 1929, the New York stock market crashed. Within one week, investors lost 40 percent of their capital. By 1932, the market had lost 89 percent of its value, and the U.S. economy entered the Great Depression. The economic hard times would last for nearly two decades and affect nearly all Americans. The 1930s also brought environmental devastation to much of the Great Plains region from Texas to the Canadian border and westward to the Rocky Mountains. Year after year, rain was scarce, and moisture-starved crops and livestock herds suffered. Soils were stripped from the land, creating violent dust storms that turned day into night. During this "dust bowl" era, nearly half a million people left their land and migrated. Most of them moved westward to California or elsewhere. It would take decades before the region—America's wheat-and-livestock-producing agricultural heartland—would return to its former level of productivity.

No sooner had the country begun a slow recovery from the Great Depression and dust bowl era than storm clouds once again started to form. In 1939, war began in Europe and soon spread like wildfire as it engaged Allied (friendly) or Axis (hostile) forces. It even spread to eastern Asia. For a time, the United States watched from the sidelines. On December 7, 1941, the Japanese bombed the U.S. military base in Pearl Harbor, Hawaii. The American response was swift and decisive.

By the war's end in 1945, U.S. military forces had played a leading role in securing the victory for itself and its allies. An estimated 72 million people died in the war, including perhaps 420,000 Americans.

THE UNITED STATES EMERGES AS A GLOBAL POWERHOUSE

After World War II, it became apparent that the United States had emerged as the world's leading economic and military power. The latter position, of course, was challenged by the Soviet Union during the "cold war" period, which lasted from 1947 until the USSR politically disintegrated in 1991. During this period, the two countries challenged one another ideologically, politically, militarily, and in many other ways—including in the race to outer space. Ultimately, in 1991, the Soviet Union and its Communist government collapsed, leaving the United States as the world's lone powerhouse. At the dawn of the new millennium, the country faces many challenges, but there are numerous reasons for optimism as you will learn in the next three chapters, which discuss the country's people and culture, government and political system, and economy.

4

People
and Culture

Give me your tired, your poor,
Your huddled masses yearning to breathe free,
The wretched refuse of your teeming shore. . . .

These lines, part of a poem written by Emma Lazarus, appear on the Statue of Liberty. They offer a very appropriate introduction to this chapter on the American population. The United States has been and continues to be a grand human experiment conducted on a colossal scale. It has often been called a "country of immigrants," people who arrived from many distant lands in pursuit of a better life. By and large, their faith in the "American dream" was rewarded with good fortune, although for some it involved a long struggle and much sacrifice. Of course, the newcomers arrived in and rapidly took control of a land already long occupied by native peoples. Today, however, the majority population is of European ancestry.

From 1886 to 1954, the Statue of Liberty served as a symbol of freedom to immigrants who entered New York Harbor on their way to their new home in the United States. The statue was presented as a gift by France to mark the centennial of the founding of the United States.

With more than 300 million people, the United States ranks third in population behind China and India, yet with an area of 3.8 million square miles (9.8 million square kilometers), the country—unlike its counterparts with high populations—is not crowded. In fact, the population density of about 80 people per square mile (30 per square kilometer) is well below the world average of about 115 (44), and 90 percent of all Americans live in less than 10 percent of the country's area! Space, good farmland, and other natural resources are abundant.

No country comes close to matching the United States in terms of human mobility. In fact, the average American moves about 12 times. Socioeconomically, few countries offer a greater opportunity for individual advancement regardless of racial, ethnic, religious, economic, or other background. The country's population is a mosaic of people who have come from every country on Earth. In doing so, the population represents the world's most ethnically diverse society in terms of ancestral "roots." Despite this great diversity, the United States has been and continues to be much more a cultural "melting pot" than a "salad bowl." Most Americans, regardless of ethnic, racial, or geographic origin, proudly think of themselves as "Americans," without a hyphenated tie to their ancestral homeland. Cultural assimilation and social integration—although slower and more difficult for some than for others—has characterized the grand American experiment.

POPULATION DATA AND THEIR IMPORTANCE

Demography is the science devoted to the statistical study of the human population. Demographic data are obtained primarily through a periodic census, a country's single most important source of information about its people. In the United States, a census is a constitutional requirement, and one has been taken every decade (in years that end in 0) since 1790. Districts of the 435 members of the U.S. House of Representatives are determined on the basis of population. California, the most populous state, has 53 members in that governing body, whereas seven states have only a single representative. Every 10 years, some states can lose and others gain seats in Congress based on new census data.

A census involves much more than a "head count." It provides a detailed statistical profile about a country's population. To get some idea of how detailed the information is, you can go to www.census.gov and note the great number of different categories. Just for fun, go to "American Factfinder." When it opens, enter your home community and state in the space provided. You contribute to not one, but many statistics!

The U.S. population is approximately 301 million (as of mid-2007) and is growing at an annual rate of about 1.2 percent per year. The rate of natural increase is about 0.9 percent, meaning that three-fourths of the growth is from the number of births compared to deaths. The other one-fourth is from immigration, both legal and undocumented. Today, the total fertility rate (TFR), or number of children to which a woman gives birth, has dropped below the replacement level of 2.1. This means that, if the country's population is going to continue to grow, either the birthrate must increase or the void must be filled by immigration. Experts believe that immigration will, indeed, continue at a rapid pace. They project a 40 percent increase in the U.S. population—to 420 million—by 2050 if the current rate of annual gain continues.

HUMAN RESOURCES

Cultural geographers have long recognized that a healthy, well-educated, productive population can and should be a country's most important resource. In this regard, the United States is extremely fortunate. For the most part, its more than 300 million people are healthy. Life expectancy at birth is 78 years, 75 for males and 81 for females. This is slightly longer than the average in the developed world and much higher than that of the world's less developed countries. The United States also has a high rate of literacy: 99 percent. Eighty percent of the population over 15 years of age has a high school education, and nearly 25 percent are college graduates. If a country is to be successful in a highly competitive postindustrial economy that involves skilled services, information exchange, and global networking, it is essential that its citizens be well educated.

As is true in nearly all countries in the developed world, America's population is aging. When births decline and life expectancy increases, a population ages. Currently, the average age in the United States is about 37 years and is increasing. Nearly 13 percent of the population is 65 years of age or older.

An aging population creates several problems. First, there are fewer young people to join the workforce. This is particularly critical at the entry level with lower-paying jobs. Second, an aging population requires increasingly costly medical attention and facilities. Finally, an aging population means more retirees who need retirement facilities and will be drawing on retirement financial packages such as social security. In each case, an added burden is placed on the nation's economy.

With declining fertility rates and an aging population, the most obvious solution to the problems is to increase immigration quotas. Currently, the United States not only accepts more immigrants than any other country, it receives more people than the rest of the world combined! Immigration can be a double-edged sword, both solving and causing problems. The nation's economic prosperity increasingly depends on immigrant labor. Furthermore, there is little to suggest that this dependence will do anything but increase during coming decades. According to various sources, however, an estimated 11 to 13 million immigrants, or nearly 4 percent of the country's total population, are in the country illegally. Immigration is one of the most challenging and hotly debated issues facing the country's political leaders.

SETTLEMENT

Settlements patterns—the distribution of people within a defined area—are among the most revealing of all geographic conditions. They help tell us not only where people choose to live, but, often, why. Some areas, of course, are extremely crowded, whereas others remain almost vacant. Initially, most European settlement hugged the eastern seaboard. Gradually, it spread southward and westward into the Ohio and Mississippi valleys, the Great Lakes region, and adjacent areas. In the mid-nineteenth century, the country's interior was leapfrogged as thousands of people migrated to the West Coast in pursuit of gold and, later, good farmland, a pleasant climate, and other

As evident on this NASA map of the "United States at Night," the majority of Americans live along the country's eastern and western seaboards. Americans have traditionally been tied to the ocean; in fact, nearly 80 percent of the country's citizens live within 200 miles of the coast.

attractions. Other than latecomer states Alaska and Hawaii, the nation's "last frontier" was the central and western interior. Much of this region was not settled until the late 1800s.

Location, Location, Location

Location—where a place is and what it has to offer—is the primary factor that influences where people decide to settle. Traditionally, economic conditions have been the primary determinant of where people choose to settle. They search for places where a decent living can be made for themselves and their families. Good farmland and other resources such as dense woodlands for timber or minerals for mining drew many settlers, as did streams that provided freshwater, easy navigation, and perhaps a site for water-powered flour, lumber, or other mills. In time, towns along railroads and, later, highways or around natural harbors grew economically, offered jobs, and attracted settlers. Through time, as economic, social, and technological changes occurred, perceptions of good (and bad) places to live also changed. Settlement, after all, is not spread evenly across the country, as can be seen on the "United States at Night" map. How might such great differences in settlement and population density be explained?

The Attraction of Water

An estimated 60 percent of all Americans live in counties that border the Atlantic or Pacific ocean or the Great Lakes, and about 80 percent live within 200 miles of these waters. Clearly, Americans are attracted to oceans, lakes, and rivers. Think for a moment about the number of ways in which you use (directly or indirectly) water every day. Water is essential to life, and the average American uses approximately 400 gallons daily. It also offers the least expensive medium for surface transportation. Water is an essential resource for many industries, and 15 percent of all American agriculture is irrigated, a figure that jumps to 85 percent in the dry Western states. More recently, people have flocked to lakeshores and seacoasts because of the scenic and recreational amenities they offer. As was noted in Chapter 2, the importance of water to a place is often suggested by its name. In addition to the terms mentioned previously, other names that suggest the importance of water include *bridge, ferry, ford, mill, portage,* and *well.*

Because natural harbors offer access to all lands that border the global sea, many cities were located around them and grew primarily because of their seaport function. On the Atlantic Coast, Boston; New York; Philadelphia; Charleston, South Carolina; Savannah, Georgia; and Jacksonville and Miami, Florida grew as major port cities. Along the Pacific Coast, San Diego, San Francisco, Seattle, and Anchorage owe much of their growth to their port function. On the Great Lakes, which have shipping access to the Atlantic Ocean, Buffalo, New York; Cleveland, Ohio; Detroit, Michigan; Chicago, Illinois; Milwaukee, Wisconsin; and Duluth, Minnesota; all grew as inland port cities. In addition, the aforementioned New Orleans; Memphis, Tennessee; St.

Louis, Missouri; and Minneapolis–St. Paul grew as ports on the Mississippi River. Upstream, Cincinnati, Ohio and Pittsburgh flourished on the Ohio River, as did Kansas City, Missouri and Omaha on the Missouri. Portland, Oregon, is on the Columbia River. Hundreds of smaller communities throughout the United States also owe their origin and growth to a riverside location.

In arid portions of the western United States, including much of California, most settlement occurred at an oasis site—a location where freshwater was available from a stream, lake, or groundwater source. Some communities outgrew their available water supply and were forced to look elsewhere in order to thrive or even survive. Most of southern California obtains its water supply from elsewhere—the Colorado River or streams that flow from the Sierra Nevada. This makes the region highly vulnerable to any event or condition that might limit the flow of water, a situation much like someone on a life-support system. In the desert Southwest, booming Phoenix, Tucson, and Las Vegas are among the country's fastest-growing metropolitan areas, yet nearly all of their growth depends on water diverted from the Colorado River. In the future, assuming that the region's population continues to grow, ensuring an adequate water supply will be the arid West's greatest challenge.

Fertile Farmland

Farming is essential to human survival—we must eat—and much of farming depends on good soil and its cultivation. The United States is blessed with some of the world's best farmland. Vast areas of flat land with good soil and adequate moisture provide the foundation on which the world's most productive agricultural economy was developed. From the very beginning of European settlement, people were drawn to good farmland. Fertile alluvial (stream-deposited) soils drew settlers inland across the broad Atlantic and Gulf coastal plains and inland along river valleys and into broad basins.

In 1862, the U.S. government took a very bold step by passing the Homestead Act, which offered free land in the country's interior to people who were willing to settle and develop it. Hundreds of thousands of people took advantage of the opportunity, swelling the population of the Interior Lowlands and Great Plains. Interestingly, much of this land could not be farmed until the steel-tipped, moldboard plow was developed by John Deere in the mid-nineteenth century. The steel tip could break the thick sod and turn the soil so it could be tilled. Later, thousands of settlers trekked westward to settle and farm the fertile Central Valley of California, Oregon's Willamette Valley, and Washington's Puget Sound and Palouse regions.

Improved Access

The phrase "build it and they will come" certainly holds true for the impact that highways and railroads have had on settlement. Between the Appalachian Mountains and the Pacific Coast (excluding Alaska and Hawaii), it is estimated that about 80 percent of all permanent communities owe their origin to railroads. Many cities, including Chicago and St. Louis, grew as major railroad transportation centers. The automobile age began in the early 1900s, following the coming of the railroads by up to half a century in some places. Whereas people were drawn to railroads, just the opposite was true in regard to highways. Highways, at least during the early decades of automotive transportation, tended to serve already-existing populations. This changed somewhat with the development of the Interstate Highway System that was begun during the 1950s.

Other Influences on Settlement

Many other factors have influenced where Americans live, now as in the past. Hundreds of communities, scattered throughout nearly every state, owe their origin to some primary industry such as mining, fishing, or logging. Such centers often experience what can best be called a "boom-and-bust" economy. The West, for example, has thousands of "ghost towns" that were once thriving mining camps. Many such communities, however, have experienced a rebirth. Because they occupy scenic locations, are of historical interest, or are ideal sites for some recreational activity, such as skiing or fishing, they have become tourist centers. Once again, place names often provide a clue to a community's origin. Dozens of towns and cities have *fort, university* or *college,* or some other term that identifies a founding function. Many cities, such as Washington, D.C., developed as seats of government.

Changing Patterns of Settlement

Americans have always been "on the go." Through time, however, ideas of *where* they want to live have changed greatly. As a result, there have been some remarkable changes in the country's settlement patterns as populations shift from place to place. That millions of Americans followed nineteenth-century newspaper editor Horace Greeley's advice to "Go West, young man, go West!" is evident by the westward shift through time of the "Mean Center of the United States Population." In 1790, the mean center was located in Kent County, on Maryland's Eastern Shore. One hundred years later, in 1890, it had moved west to Decatur County, in southeastern Indiana. And, most recently, in 2000, it was located in south-central Missouri's Phelps County.

There have been many other shifts. At one time, most Americans were rural. During the past century, however, tens of millions of people have participated in a massive rural-to-urban migration. Today, in fact, nearly 80 percent of all Americans reside in urban centers (communities with more than 2,500 residents). Long ago, people found that they could no longer make an adequate living on a small family farm. Cities, however, offered a variety of wage-paying employment opportunities. Schools, health care, and entertainment were better, as were shopping options and other services. There were libraries, museums, and art galleries and also organized sports, opera halls, and restaurants.

As urban transportation facilities improved, people could commute to work. They could live at the city's edge and still

Today, more than 80 percent of Americans live in urban centers, including San Antonio, Texas, which, according to the 2000 U.S. Census, was the ninth-largest city in the country. Of the nation's 10 largest cities, San Antonio had the second-largest growth rate (behind Phoenix) between 2000 and 2002.

work "downtown." This resulted in what urban geographers call the urban-to-fringe migration that created *suburbia*. Suburbs were removed from the congestion, pollution, and growing decay of urban centers, and they also offered a more open and natural landscape. Today, many people are moving even farther out from the urban center to exurban locations. *Exurbia* is simply defined as "beyond the suburbs." For some commuters, it may be many miles beyond. The author knows a number of people who have a daily commute of 50 to 100 miles or more to work each way. One major attraction of exurbia is that, in many locations, real estate sells or rents for a small fraction of its cost in the city or suburbs.

Another mass migration has occurred during the past half century. Millions of people have fled the Rust Belt or Snow Belt of the Northeast and have moved to the warmer Sun Belt of the South and Southwest, an area that stretches from Virginia to southern California. During the 1960s, effective and relatively inexpensive air-conditioning was developed. It made comfortable living possible despite the scorching temperatures of the desert Southwest and soggy heat and humidity of the South. Many other factors were involved. Property, taxes, and other costs of living were much less expensive in the Sun Belt states. Businesses were attracted by lower wages, a large labor pool, lower taxes, and other lucrative incentives.

During recent decades, major changes in American culture and society have contributed to still another major shift in settlement. Until recently, people had little choice but to live where they could make a living. In retirement, they lived close to family members who cared for them during their twilight years. Today, millions of people make their livings from jobs that are not tied to one place (for example, a large industrial city). They can live where they want, rather than need, to reside. Some are self-employed; they may be artists, writers, musicians, or craftsmen. Others need only a computer to do their jobs successfully. These are the kinds of changes made possible as American society has moved from an industrial economy to a postindustrial service-based economy. In addition, and really for the first time in history, many retirees can count on their own savings and retirement programs, including social security, to retire where they like.

The result of these changes is that millions of people have chosen to settle in "amenity" locations. These are places that offer exceptional scenery, a pleasant climate, varied recreational opportunities, or some other amenity that attracts people. Sea-coasts, mountainous areas, and lakes are examples of such locations. As recently as the 1950s, most coastal areas of the country, with the exception of major port cities or resort centers enjoyed by the extremely wealthy, had very sparse settlement. Economically, there was nothing to do. The Appalachians and Ozarks were remote, isolated, run-down centers of extreme poverty and home to little more than socially scorned "hillbillies." The Mountain West was dotted with once-prosperous mining centers whose empty streets and decaying structures stood as stark reminders of a more prosperous past. Amazingly, within the past half century there has been a complete turnaround. Today, coastal areas, mountain regions, and historical centers—which once offered the nation's cheapest property and lowest population densities—are booming. Population is soaring and property values are now some of the nation's highest.

If a country is to achieve the stability needed for its population to prosper, it must have a government that is responsive to its people and their needs. It also must have a strong and diverse economy. The United States has been and continues to be extremely fortunate. It is blessed to have both a responsive and enduring political system and a vibrant and diverse economy. How the country has prospered politically and economically is the topic of the next two chapters.

5

Government and Politics

E pluribus unum is perhaps the best-known motto of the United States of America. Translated from Latin, it means "From many, one," or "Out of many, one." In working to achieve this goal, the nation's Founding Fathers and subsequent leaders faced a challenge of herculean dimensions. You have already learned that, from the very beginning, this land has been home to people of extremely diverse ethnicity, language, religion, social background, and political orientation. The colonial population was sharply divided into 13 political units, each of which was fiercely proud and semi-independent, although under British political domination. In this chapter, you will learn how the United States became a strong and unified country guided by a constitution that would satisfy the great majority of its citizens.

Political decisions and government affect nearly every aspect of our lives and range in scope from local ordinances to national laws.

It is human nature to complain about the government, and Americans often fail to realize the advantages they have. Few countries on Earth have a government that is more responsible, responsive, or enduring than that of the United States. For this, Americans are extremely fortunate.

Citizens are protected by laws, many of which strongly influence individual actions as well as those of society as a whole. Americans benefit from countless government services that range from police and fire protection to mail delivery, health care, and social security for the elderly. Public facilities are everywhere in the form of roads and highways, government buildings, monuments, and other structures. Land is divided by government survey systems, and both ownership and possible limitations on land use are established by laws that relate to property and zoning. Public lands—including national parks, monuments, forests, historical sites, and other areas—are set aside, protected, and maintained for public use and enjoyment. The United States has the world's strongest military, located on many bases. It has protected America's shores from foreign invasion and played a leading role in ending two major world wars. It also was instrumental in ending the cold war between the United States and the Soviet Union.

Governments impose restrictions on the use of land and other natural resources through laws regarding forestry, grazing, farming, mining, use of wetlands, hunting and fishing, and numerous other activities. Water and soil resources also are protected by both federal and local laws. Zoning restrictions limit the use of land in urban and most rural areas. Such restrictions are designed to protect the environment, as well as the well-being of citizens.

Early immigrants to the United States came for a variety of reasons. Some were searching for riches and opportunity. Others had been persecuted because of their religion or because of oppressive authoritarian governments. Still others chose to come as indentured servants, and some were forced to come as slaves. With this diverse mixture of new Americans, there was great fear of a strong central government. Europe was infested with monarchies that were sometimes benevolent and sometimes not. Authority had long been vested in the king or queen in powerful countries such as England, France, Spain, Portugal, and the Netherlands and in the tsar in Russia. The royal authority was believed by many to have been conferred by God. As a result, these monarchs often placed themselves above the laws that common people had to follow.

FORMING A GOVERNMENT

A government in which certain people are above the law is referred to as the "rule of man." A more desirable situation exists when all citizens, even leaders, are subject to laws. This is referred to as the "rule of law." Many of the immigrants who arrived in the New World before America became independent had fled from countries where the rule of man was exercised. This rule was often harsh and unfair and did not allow for upward social mobility, religious freedom, and many other basic rights. This meant that most early European Americans were very reluctant to create a strong central government for the newly independent United States.

Instead, early colonists experimented with a variety of governing structures. Some colonies tried to enforce established religions. Others wanted rights that had been granted in England under the Magna Carta. Still others wanted separation of powers so that no one part of the government became too strong. Colonists tried these and other ideas during the colonial era, and the lessons learned were used to create the U.S. government. A key idea that emerged from the colonial era was the notion of representative governments. This meant that people elected representatives to carry forward citizen issues and to protect the interests of the voters. This idea was a key element in the creation of the U.S. government and those of the various states.

At the time that America won independence, the early colonies were self-governing and more like independent countries than the states they would later become. Small states also feared the power of big states. Primarily because of these factors and the continuing wariness about strong central governments, the 13 original colonies' first attempt at a national government was a system provided by the Articles of Confederation in 1776 in which there was a unified country with a weak national government. Each state retained sovereignty and powers, and the central government got what was left over. In practice, the leftovers were not enough for the young nation to move forward effectively and as a unified country. Major problems, including the national government's inability to tax or regulate trade and conflicts and affairs between states and the lack of power over citizens, quickly emerged. The latter became an issue because the state governments had retained the primary authority over citizens. By the mid-1780s, many key American leaders such as James Madison and Alexander Hamilton had become very dissatisfied with the government under the Articles of Confederation and initiated efforts to move forward with a new government.

In 1786, Madison and others determined that a convention should be established and convened with the express purpose of developing a new constitution. The new constitution would have a stronger central government but would also preserve important rights for the states. The Constitutional Convention met in Philadelphia in the summer of 1787. Fifty-five representatives came from throughout the colonies and included important men such as George Washington, George Mason, James Madison, Alexander Hamilton, and Benjamin Franklin. Of the 55 attendees at the Philadelphia convention, 39 later signed the Constitution. Some, like George Mason, did not sign the document. He believed that the Constitution should have a Bill of Rights and that senators should be elected rather than appointed by state legislatures as the original Constitution stated. Both of Mason's ideas would later be incorporated into the Constitution through amendments.

The Constitutional Convention convened in Philadelphia during the summer of 1787 to create a new government for the United States after its victory over Great Britain in the American Revolution. Here, 39 of the 55 delegates are depicted in *Scene at the Signing of the Constitution of the United States,* Howard Chandler Christy's famous rendition of the historic event.

THE CONSTITUTION

The constitution that was created during the hot summer of 1787 was developed by a diverse group of men that consisted of farmers, military men, politicians, businessmen, statesmen, and schemers. Their average age was only 42, and they came from throughout the colonies to design a better government for the

newly independent country. Constitutions can be very important documents: They can serve as vital living contracts—the
highest law in the country—between citizens and their governments. If ignored or trampled by leaders who are not held
accountable, however, constitutions can become meaningless
pieces of paper. Fortunately, the framers of the U.S. Constitution were serious-minded men who wanted a strong central
government with separation of powers and checks and balances on the powers of important leaders and institutions.

To this end, the Constitution's framers developed three
branches of government: the executive, legislative, and judicial
branches. Each not only had powers identified in the Constitution but also had its powers checked by the other branches. The
executive branch is headed by the president, and this section of
the government is charged with enforcing the law and adminis-
tering government. The legislative branch, which is Congress, was
established with two houses, the Senate and the House of Representatives. This branch is responsible for making laws for the
country. The judicial branch serves as the system of justice, and
the U.S. Supreme Court is the highest court. The judicial branch
is responsible for interpreting the laws of the United States.

As designed by the framers, there were many checks and
balances established to keep the separation of powers strong
and to keep any one branch from becoming too dominant.
For example, many positions that require appointments by
the president, such as cabinet posts or ambassadors, must be
approved by Congress. Congress establishes the budget and
laws but the president can veto these bills. Congress, however,
can override vetoes with a two-thirds majority vote in both
houses. Another example is Supreme Court justices: They are
appointed by the president but must be confirmed by Congress. In a countercheck, laws or administrative policies that are
determined by the U.S. Supreme Court to be unconstitutional
will be thrown out. Thus, the judicial branch also has checks
on the other two branches. Rogue judges or presidents can be

impeached and removed by Congress. The checks and balances contained in the Constitution are many, and they have served their purpose well through time.

Various attempts have been made by one branch of government or another to usurp additional powers, but most have been successfully resisted. For example, in the mid-twentieth century, President Franklin Roosevelt wasn't getting the court decisions he wanted. He came forward with a court-packing scheme designed to increase the court from 9 to 15 justices. This effort failed, as did President Richard Nixon's attempt to hide information about the Watergate break-in during his term in office. The Supreme Court unanimously voted to have him turn over the transcripts of tapes that were important in the investigation of the break-in and cover-up. The repeated tests of the U.S. Constitution produced a republic that has lasted for more than two centuries, and few changes have been made in the original document. Clearly, the framers were brilliant visionaries.

The only changes to the Constitution come in the form of amendments. These can be made by a lengthy and difficult process. To amend the U.S. Constitution first requires either a two-thirds vote of both houses of Congress or of state legislatures (or state conventions) to propose an amendment. The proposed amendment then must be ratified (approved) by three-fourths of the states through either the state legislatures or state conventions. With this challenging process, changes to the U.S. Constitution are infrequent when compared with those of most other countries.

From the implementation of the Constitution in 1789 until the publication of this book, only 27 amendments have been ratified. The first 10, called the Bill of Rights, were adopted immediately after the Constitution was implemented, when James Madison introduced them into the House of Representatives. The other 17 amendments have been the only changes to the Constitution in more than 200 years. This is less than one change every 13 years. The last was adopted in 1992.

The U.S. Constitution is today regarded as one of the most amazing and enduring documents in the world. Created more than two centuries ago, it has survived a variety of challenges, including westward expansion; the addition of new states; involvement in numerous wars, including the Civil War; and the end of slavery. It has also endured countless advances in technology, staggering population and economic growth, the expansion of civil rights, the space age, and terrorism. After elections, changes in political leadership are made smoothly, and the nation has survived the shock of presidential impeachments and even assassinations. Not only has the document survived, but its flexibility and the foresight it has provided have allowed the country to become the leading economic and military power in the world today.

A NATION GROWS

Countries and organisms have much in common: They can grow, remain steady, or wither away. Europeans established a tenuous colonial toehold along the eastern seaboard four centuries ago, and, eventually, what was to become the United States grew to span the North American continent from the Atlantic Ocean to the shores of the Pacific and beyond to Alaska and Hawaii. Like a giant picture puzzle, this vast country came together piece by piece.

In 1776, the United States of America was composed of the 13 former colonies. These lands were sandwiched between the Atlantic Coast and the Appalachian Mountains and extended from Maine to Georgia. By 1783, the country's territory had expanded to include nearly all of the area located east of the Mississippi River. Two decades later, in 1803, the Louisiana Purchase added nearly 828,000 square miles (2,100,000 square kilometers) of territory that roughly coincided with the interior one-third of the present-day country. For this land, France received about three cents per acre (seven cents per hectare) in what certainly ranks as one of the best real estate bargains of all time! The remainder of the West was gradually acquired from Spain or Mexico between 1819 and 1853. Two large pieces of the puzzle, the Pacific Northwest (Oregon Territory) and much of the Southwest, were both added in 1846. Finally, with the Gadsden Purchase of 1853, the territory occupied by the 48 adjoining states was all under the U.S. flag.

The final two pieces of the U.S. map puzzle to fall into place were Alaska and Hawaii. Alaska was purchased from Russia in 1867 for $7.2 million, or about two cents per acre (five cents per hectare)! Many Americans were very critical of the purchase, which came to be known as "Seward's Folly" (after U.S. Secretary of State William H. Seward, who brokered the purchase). History, however, has smiled kindly on Seward's bold decision, because today Alaska contributes more revenue to the U.S. economy *each day* than it originally cost! Hawaii was annexed in 1898. Not until 1959 did Alaska and Hawaii became the forty-ninth and fiftieth stars on the U.S. flag, respectively. In pursuit of its *manifest destiny*—the belief held by Americans that it was their "right" to expand from "sea to shining sea"—the United States faced many obstacles. Physical problems included huge distances, harsh weather (frigid cold in the winter and scorching heat in the summer), and rugged terrain that included soaring mountain barriers. Most of the land already was claimed by Spain, France, Mexico, or Russia, and, of course, it had been occupied for thousands of years by native peoples to whom it was home.

POLITICAL IMPRINT ON THE LANDSCAPE

Think for a moment about your surrounding landscape, or the "look of the land." How much of what you see is a part of the political cultural landscape? Actually, nearly everything you see has been affected in some way by political decisions. Public schools are paid for by taxes, the flags that wave above the buildings represent the state and nation, the street is public, and cars are licensed by state and county. Transportation (vehicle, rail, air, pipeline, and other) and communications that reach your community are government licensed and regulated. Your community no doubt has a number of public buildings, such as a city hall, a post office, and a number of other local, county, state, and federal office buildings (depending on the size and function of your community). Outside of the community, much of the land may be owned by the state or the federal government. Everywhere you look, the imprint of government is etched on the landscape.

The author has arbitrarily selected six acts of Congress that have had a profound effect on the nation's cultural landscape. There are, of course, many more.

Public Lands Acts (various dates)

The United States is a huge country, and much of it belongs to the public. In fact, about 765 million acres (310 million hectares)—nearly one-third of the total U.S. land area—is publicly owned! About 653 million acres (264 million hectares), or almost 29 percent of the country's total land area, is controlled by the federal government. The figure would be much higher if city-, county-, and state-owned lands were included in this tally. In Alaska and Nevada, about 90 percent of the land is government owned. Federal lands fall within dozens of categories that range from parks and wilderness areas to Indian Trust lands, national forests and grasslands, and military bases, to name but a few. As elements of the cultural landscape, they have numerous "appearances." If there is a common thread that unites most of them, however, it is the restriction of development and thereby protection of lands for public use and enjoyment.

Land Ordinance Survey (1785)

Perhaps more than any other political element, land survey systems impose a unique imprint on the land. In most of the eastern and southeastern United States, the landscape has a very irregular pattern. Surveying there was by a "metes-and-bounds"

The federal government administers approximately 653 million acres of land in the United States, which is about 30 percent of the nation's area. Here, two cyclists ride along the 13-mile-long scenic drive at Red Rock Canyon National Conservation Area in Nevada's Mojave Desert, which is administered by the Bureau of Land Management.

system. There is little "order" to the land: Roads seem to wander aimlessly, fields are irregular in shape, and few features are oriented in the cardinal directions. By the time the Midwest and West were settled, however, this pattern had changed.

The Land Ordinance Survey of 1785 created the American rectangular survey system, which gave rise to a very orderly "checkerboard" system of land division. Nearly all cultural features are oriented in cardinal directions—that is, roads, community layouts, buildings, land holdings, fields, and nearly everything else is built "square" to north, south, east, or west. Where justified by population and land use, roads are spaced at one-mile intervals, a feature that adds to a uniform (and some would say "boring") landscape. In a few locations, Spanish land grants and the French long lot system also contributed to distinctive land division patterns.

Homestead Act (1862)

When traveling in the United States, many foreigners are amazed at the dispersed rural settlement that is so commonplace in the Midwest and much of the West. People live far from one another rather than in rural villages as is the case throughout most of the world. In 1862, the United States passed the Homestead Act, which was responsible for this uniquely American rural settlement pattern. The act granted homesteaders a title to 160 acres (about 65 hectares; a quarter section, or one-fourth of a square mile) of largely undeveloped land. There were few stipulations other than that the person had to be 21 years of age, build a small house on the land, and live on and develop the homestead for a period of five years. Those in a hurry could even buy the land on which they settled for $1.25 per acre ($2.50 per hectare) after only one year of successful homesteading. Lured by the "free" land, thousands of people moved westward, settled un(der)developed lands, engaged in farming, and lived scattered throughout the countryside.

Railroad Federal Land Grants (1862–1871)

As the nation began to move westward toward its vast and largely undeveloped frontier, it was widely recognized that rail linkages must be built if the region was to grow economically. Some settlers already were moving to the eastern margins of the western frontier, drawn by the lure of free land. In order to help defray the high cost of railroad building, Congress passed the Pacific Railway Act in 1862. This gave the Union Pacific and Central Pacific (see Chapter 3 for details) railroads a 400-foot right of way, plus 10 square miles (25.9 square kilometers) of land for every mile (1.61 kilometers) of track built. Subsequently, other railroads received similar incentives.

It is difficult to imagine what America would be like had it not been for the dense network of railroads that provided access to nearly every developed part of the country. Because of the lands granted to them, the railroads platted (mapped the plan for) and spurred development of thousands of communities along their routes. In fact, in the nation's heartland, up to 90 percent of all communities were established in this way. In much of the Midwest, it was determined that the railroad "carrying capacity" of the population and economy could support a small rural community located along the tracks at intervals of six to eight miles. This spacing is based on the fact that a farmer could drive his horse- or oxen-drawn wagon to town a distance of three to four miles each way and return home in time to do the evening chores. Every 40 to 70 miles, a larger community grew to serve the railroad and its various functions. This pattern can be seen on any detailed map that shows where railroads were located a century ago.

National Park Service (1916)

America is home to countless natural, historical, and cultural treasures. Long ago, many of the country's leaders realized that they should be protected from random development and be preserved for all people to enjoy. Yellowstone became the nation's (and the world's) first national park in 1872, but it was not until 1916 that the National Park Service was created. Today, this branch of the government oversees 390 national sites. They include 58 national parks and 230 other monuments, historical parks, memorials, seashores, trails, and other features. No other country comes close to matching the United States in protecting its natural and cultural heritage for public enjoyment and future generations.

Federal-Aid Highway Act (1956)

Imagine driving across the United States on a two-lane highway! In terms of speed and safety of travel and convenience, the 1956 legislation that created the Interstate Highway System was a momentous act. Today, an integrated network of "superhighways" crisscrosses the country. The impact of interstate highways has influenced much more than travel alone. In many states, it has altered population, settlement, and cultural landscape. As a general rule, communities on or near the highways are thriving, whereas those without easy interstate access are stagnant or even declining. In many instances, the "old" town has withered as a "new" commercial area has sprouted up near the highway. These adjustments have altered the cultural landscape, as have the strips of development that follow suburban interstate corridors, which range from shopping malls to warehouses and firms that depend heavily on interstate trucking. There are also the omnipresent motels, restaurants, gas stations, and convenience stores found clustered around many exits.

GOVERNMENT AND ECONOMIC DEVELOPMENT

Government plays a very critical role in a nation's economy. Simply stated, good government is the foundation on which a strong economy can build. (The opposite, of course, also is true.) In the United States, a government-supported free market (capitalist) economy has led to the country's widespread prosperity. Establishing and promoting economic policy, however, is only one of many ways in which the government supports economic development. Most citizens and businesses depend on reliable government-built, -supported, or -regulated transportation and communication. Government plays a very important role in agriculture, industry, and other businesses. From resource exploitation to marketing, production to sales, waste disposal to taxation, or labor laws to import-export controls, the government exerts a strong influence.

The following chapter investigates how the United States has become the world's greatest economic powerhouse.

6

The United States' Economy

With an annual gross national product (GNP) of about $13 trillion in 2006, the United States is the world's largest and most powerful economy by a wide margin. By any measure, the country is an economic giant. In fact, it is responsible for about 30 percent of all of the world's economic production and services! To place the country's economic strength in perspective, were California an independent country, it would be the world's fifth-ranking economic power! Texas and New York would be close behind, also in the top 10.

Many factors contribute to a country's economic development, and the United States has benefited from several. The country's location is in the easily developed temperate midlatitudes but has extremities that extend into both the tropics and the arctic. Because of this environmental diversity, the United States can engage in any climate-dependent economic activity. The country is strategically positioned between the world's largest populations and the thriving economies of Europe and East Asia. It faces three oceans that allow inexpensive access to world resources and markets, as well as offering protection for much of the country's periphery. Economic growth also has been spurred by the country's wealth of natural resources, including metals and fuels, productive and diverse ecosystems, abundant water and fertile soils, and many other elements that are essential to economic growth.

Humans also are important resources. No country can match the United States in terms of its well-educated, skilled, healthy, and hardworking labor force. Unlike many countries, the United States has ample space for future human settlement and economic development. As has already been emphasized elsewhere, the economic system—the means of production, the variety and efficiency of services, and the ways in which wealth is distributed—and a stable government have been the keys to more than two centuries of prosperity. In a free market economy, individuals and businesses can pursue their economic goals with little government interference.

FOUNDATIONS OF ECONOMIC DEVELOPMENT

Many factors influence a nation's level of economic well-being. You already have seen how vital a role government plays in this process, but that is only one of many pieces of a much larger economic picture. It may seem that a vast area of land, a wealth of natural resources, and a large population would be keys to strong economic development, but a survey of the world's countries clearly shows that none of these factors alone can ensure a strong economy. Ultimately, the most important key to economic development is a people's cultural system. Space and natural elements are of no value until they are used by humans. Needs, perceptions, and values all play an important role, as do available capital and technology, human resources, the economic system, laws and customs, and a number of other cultural factors.

Environmental Resources

Natural resources are things in nature that people use. Environmental resources can and often do provide a solid foundation for economic development. Former Chinese leader Mao Tse-tung once suggested that there is no such thing as unproductive lands; rather, there are only unproductive people. The United States is extremely fortunate in having a varied and abundant natural endowment, but it is the country's human resources, a stable government, and adequate capital and technology—all components of the American cultural system—that have made the country so economically successful.

As you learned in Chapter 2, no country can match America's environmental diversity or the wealth of its natural resource endowment. It has a wealth of land features, climates, natural vegetation and animal life, soils, water features, and natural resources. No country comes close to equaling the United States in terms of its quantity of productive land, either. Agriculture thrives on the country's huge expanse of relatively flat land, with adequate moisture, good soil, and a long growing season. Where nature fails to provide adequate moisture, abundant capital resources and technology make irrigation of crops possible. Because of the diverse environmental conditions in the United States, any of the world's crops or animals can be raised somewhere in the country. Huge expanses of forest support a productive logging industry, just as the oceans provide many valuable marine resources. Highlands attract tourists and retirees and also serve as giant sponges that take up and gradually release water into hundreds of streams that join to form the nation's major rivers. As you learned in Chapter 4, climate played a major role in the Snow Belt-to-Sun Belt migration of people and businesses.

The United States has been blessed with a wealth of mineral resources, as well. Mineral fuels are essential to economic growth, and the country has been able to tap vast supplies of petroleum, natural gas, coal, and uranium. Manufacturing industries have had access to huge deposits of iron ore, copper, lead, zinc, and many other metals, and the country has benefited from large stores of precious minerals, including gold, silver, platinum, and gemstones.

Culture and Economic Prosperity

Many cultural factors also have contributed to America's economic development. A strong "Protestant work ethic" was introduced by northwestern Europeans. These same people introduced the ideas and practices associated with the Industrial and Commercial revolutions that began several centuries ago in the British Isles. Once they became rooted, the ideas of manufacturing and marketing the goods produced spread rapidly along the eastern seaboard, as did the growth of early industrial cities. The important idea of a market-based economy also came from northwestern Europe. Americans have been world leaders in inventions and innovations that have made the United States the unchallenged world leader in technology. To name but a few, where would we be without electricity, telecommunications, airplanes, and the computer and Internet? These and many other developments have helped the U.S. economy become the world's strongest.

A well-integrated network of highways and railroads, airways and waterways, pipelines and transmission lines, and other distribution networks is essential to economic development. The United States is fortunate to have excellent facilities and networks in each of these vital categories. These linkages support production, distribution, and provision of services that are essential to economic growth and stability.

Many other factors also are of great importance, but a detailed list would far exceed the scope of this book. The

Located on lower Manhattan's Wall Street, the New York Stock Exchange is the largest in the world (by volume of money traded). Here, traders work on the floor of the exchange, which was founded in 1817.

financial sector, for example, is extremely complex and also essential to economic growth and stability. Banking; credit, including the use of credit cards; and the stock and commodity markets are important, as are advertising, marketing, regional and global economic alliances, and an affluent consumer-oriented society.

To be successful in today's economy, one must think globally. The price of commodities here in the United States is often influenced by events in some distant land. Conflict in the Middle East, for example, has caused an increase of the price of gasoline. Drought in China or Brazil can mean a banner year for soybean farmers in the United States, and financial problems in Japan or terrorist activity such as that which occurred in New York City on September 11, 2001, can cause staggering losses in the stock market. Many Americans are concerned about the practice of "outsourcing"—turning to foreign sources for less-costly labor, manufactured goods, and various services. All Americans benefit from lower costs, but the practice can create hardship for some workers who are unable to adapt to changing conditions. This is particularly true of many blue-collar workers who lack the education and skills to move into white-collar jobs.

TYPES OF ECONOMIC ACTIVITY

Economic activities can be divided in several ways. The classification system most commonly used by geographers is based on how people make their living and the skills or knowledge needed to adequately perform their tasks. Most jobs in the extractive industries (farming, fishing, mining, and lumbering), for example, require some skill and considerable physical labor but little formal education. Levels of schooling tend to be low, as are the incomes of most people engaged in these industries, and jobs tend to be tied to one location, as are the people who depend on them. People who work in these "primary" industries often have little awareness of the world that exists beyond their own community or area.

At the opposite extreme are workers who provide specialized services. They are educated professionals who are usually highly paid for their services. Executives, physicians, educators, research scientists, airline pilots, and many other highly skilled people fall within this category. People engaged in these activities are quite mobile. (The author, a college professor, has moved about 20 times.) Increasingly, they work in a "global arena" and must be keenly aware of events that occur throughout the world: They must think geographically. The jet age has placed nearly any city in the world within a day's reach, and telecommunications and computers have shrunk the world into one small neighborhood. We live in an "information age." Today, one can easily communicate almost instantaneously with people anywhere in the world. Perhaps more than any other factor, this has changed the way in which business is done in the new and still emerging global marketplace.

Primary Industries

Primary industries are economic activities based directly on the extraction or exploitation of natural resources. As the nation becomes more concerned about various environmental quality issues, these industries—such as logging, mining, fishing, and farming—have become increasingly subject to various legal restrictions and limitations. Today, only a small number of people, about 2 percent of the population, are engaged in primary industries, and the number continues to decline sharply.

Agriculture

Traditionally, agriculture—ranching or farming to produce food, beverage, and fiber—has been the primary industry that involves the greatest number of people; however, today, less than 1 percent of all Americans are involved in agriculture. Nonetheless, the United States is the world's greatest producer of agricultural commodities by a wide margin. Farmers have been helped by a favorable climate, fertile soils, and abundant relatively flat land suitable for large mechanized equipment. The country also has benefited from outstanding agricultural research and technology. A major step in this direction was taken by the 1862 Morrill Land-Grant Act, which created land grant colleges. These institutions

Although less than 1 percent of Americans are involved in the farming industry, agriculture plays an important role in the U.S. economy. The U.S. wine and grape industry brings in more than $162 billion annually, with the state of California leading the way. Pictured here is a Cabernet Sauvignon vineyard in Sonoma County, California.

(which often incorporate "State" in their names) place heavy emphasis on agricultural research.

Although the number of farmers and ranchers has declined steadily for nearly half a century, the size of agricultural operations has increased greatly, as has agricultural production. Today, huge farms and livestock or poultry raisers have replaced small family units. Most specialize in a single crop or type of livestock or poultry. The result has been record production that shows no sign of slowing. In fact, farmers are so successful that Americans now use 20 percent of corn in our vehicles (ethanol), rather than for livestock or in food and beverage products!

Fishing

Fishing is a troubled industry. Initially, fish, shrimp, lobsters, crabs, oysters, and other marine resources were abundant in America's waters. Today, however, overharvesting has resulted in many species becoming severely depleted. Not only is the cost of most seafood outrageously high, but many species, including salmon, shrimp, oysters, tilapia, and crawfish, are now "farmed." The demand for seafood nonetheless continues to increase. If the global sea is going to continue to be productive, international laws must be adopted and enforced to protect this fragile ecosystem and its resources.

Mineral Extraction

Mineral resources—fuels, metals, stone, and clay—have long been a backbone of American economic growth. One could even argue that the country's mineral wealth was instrumental in its rise as the world's leading economic power. Until very recently, the United States had adequate supplies of coal, petroleum, and natural gas to fuel its economy. Essential metals, including iron, lead, zinc, and copper, were abundant, as were a number of alloys and precious metals. Only during recent decades has the country been forced to rely more on foreign sources for many minerals. Many political, economic, and scientific leaders are concerned about the country's future energy supply: America has become increasingly dependent on foreign—and often politically unstable—sources for petroleum. Coal, of which huge deposits exist, is a "dirty" energy source, and its use is discouraged by many people who are concerned about environmental quality. Rich uranium deposits exist, but the idea of generating electricity with nuclear energy worries some people.

Logging

Of all primary industries, perhaps none is under greater attack by environmentalists than logging. Can you imagine, though, not having wood for building, pulp for packaging and paper, and other industrial products that depend on the logging industry? Forests once covered much of the country with the exception of lower elevations in the central and western interior. In the West, dense forests of redwood, fir, pine, spruce, and other valuable species stretched from central California northward into Alaska. Today, however, much of the lumber-grade natural timber is either gone or is growing in protected sanctuaries such as parks or federal wilderness areas. Paradoxically, during recent decades, woodlands have actually increased in area. "Tree plantations," acreages on which trees are grown as a crop, are scattered throughout the South. In the Northwest, as trees are cut, they are replaced (although it can take centuries for some trees, such as the giant redwoods, to grow to harvestable size).

Secondary Industries

Secondary industries are those that process natural resources or agricultural products. They include most types of manufacturing, the construction industries (which use stone, gravel, cement, clay, or other earthen material), food processing, and energy production. Smelting and refining, steel production, and industries that manufacture products such as petrochemicals, textiles and garments, and automobiles and aircraft fall within this category. Today, much of the world's secondary economic activity has shifted from the Western industrial world to less-developed countries. In places such as China, Indonesia, and Mexico, wages and other costs are much lower. In addition, labor and environmental laws are lax or nonexistent. Since the end of World War II, the number of Americans engaged in secondary industries has declined from about 40 percent of the workforce to about 10 percent, and the number decreases every year.

Tertiary and Other Related Activities

Today, about 84 percent of all employed Americans are engaged in tertiary or related industries, those that provide a special service of some kind. Perhaps you have heard of the "postindustrial," or "information-based," economy. This type of activity dominates the economy of all developed countries.

Approximately 84 percent of Americans are employed in tertiary, or service, industries. On the other hand, only about 10 percent of Americans are employed in secondary industries, such as factory work. Pictured here is the American Apparel factory in Los Angeles, California, one of the fastest-growing retail companies in the United States.

Many people involved in tertiary economic activities work in wholesale or retail positions. Examples include those who transport and deliver goods and those who work in sales. Teachers and professors, law enforcement officers and attorneys, physicians and nurses all work in the tertiary economic sector, as do professional athletes and other entertainers, pilots and other airline personnel, and administrators. As this sector continues to grow, it will need millions of people who are well educated, possess some useful technological skill, and are good communicators. Geographers and others in the geospatial sciences, for example, think globally, and many have mastered geographic information systems (GIS) technology and its applications. This ability is in such demand that geography and GIS rank among the very highest growth employment fields.

TRADE AND COMMERCE

How many of your possessions did you create yourself? For most of us, the answer is "none." Nearly everything we own, consume, use or come in contact with has come from someplace or someone else. Whether a stalk of celery, a stick of gum, automobile repair, or a haircut, the item or service was either produced or provided by someone other than you. It also involved transportation of either the product, or of you to the service. At various steps of the transfer, money was exchanged for the product or service. This, basically, is what trade and commerce entail.

Trade and commerce can involve something as local as a farmer growing produce and selling it at a roadside stand near his home. It also can involve a very complex series of exchanges that reach hundreds, if not thousands, of providers located throughout the global community. Your "Made in the USA" car, for example, may be manufactured by a Japanese corporation and made from components provided by dozens of countries around the world. (Just for fun, do a quick survey around your home and make a list of the items that are of foreign origin.) Obviously, the United States is unable to provide all of the goods and services that Americans consume or use. Americans produce many things in excess of our own needs, though, and this is the basis for international trade that involves exports and imports.

Not surprisingly, the United States and Canada are each other's major trading partner. In fact, more trade flows between these two countries than between any others in the world. In 1988, Canada and the United States signed the mutual Free Trade Agreement (FTA). In simplest terms, it removed high tariffs (taxes) on goods exchanged between the two countries. In 1994, Mexico was included in what became the North American Free Trade Agreement (NAFTA). In 2007, approximately 50 percent of all U.S. trade involved its two NAFTA member neighbors.

ECONOMIC CONDITIONS AND CONCERNS

The U.S. economy is the world's strongest and most stable. As mentioned previously, it produces approximately $13 trillion in goods and services annually. Most economic indicators are strong: The nation's economy is growing at about 3 to 4 percent every year, the annual rate of inflation is less than 3 percent (May 2007), unemployment is below 5 percent, and the per-capita gross domestic product is $43,500 (2006). There also are problems, however. For example, in 2007, the country carries a huge national debt, nearly $9 trillion (about $29,300 for each man, woman, and child). Also, in 2006, the country imported $765 billion more in goods and services than it exported, resulting in a huge and growing trade deficit.

As you have learned, the U.S. population is aging. As senior citizens leave the workforce, there are fewer and fewer young people to replace them. Increasingly, these jobs are filled by international workers, an estimated 11 to 13 million of whom are undocumented, or in the country illegally. As people retire, they are eligible for both social security and Medicare. Both programs are critically underfunded and will impose a huge financial burden on future workers. As the nation moves even further into the postindustrial information age, it requires an ever-increasing number of highly educated and highly skilled workers. American education, according to many experts, is

unable to meet the demand. If future generations are to compete successfully in the global economy of the twenty-first
century, they must understand the world in which they live. A
strong background in geography certainly is one step toward
achieving this goal, yet most states emphasize history, rather
than geography, in their curriculum. In this regard, it must be
remembered that a society that understands and lives a good
geography will surely leave a good history.

7

Living in the United States Today

For the majority of Americans, life is good. Few countries can match the level of health care, longevity, income, or educational attainment enjoyed by American citizens. The same can be said for the nation's transportation and communications infrastructure, services, and many other developments that Americans often take for granted. In 2006, the United States ranked eighth among the world's countries in the Human Development Index (HDI), a scale of human well-being based on a number of quality-of-life factors. From the dawn of European settlement, millions of people have successfully pursued the "American dream." Rather than being a monolithic goal, this dream assumed many forms as viewed by various individuals and groups. America was and is a land of opportunity, and the American dream remains very much alive. In answer to those who may doubt the country's commitment to diversity, the United States accepts more immigrants each year than the rest of the world's countries *combined.* In this chapter, the focus is on diversity—diversity of ethnicity and culture, of language and religion, and of land and life in the country's various subregions.

ETHNICITY

Much is heard today about America's "multicultural diversity." Actually, the country has always been culturally diverse. Native Americans represented many cultures and tribal societies; European immigrants came from numerous homelands and introduced many ways of living, although many arrived as slaves; Africans came from many locations, each with a unique culture; and, in time, people from various parts of Asia added to the rich mix. In fact, if you think about it, almost everything that Americans possess is of foreign origin! (This reality is marvelously illustrated in Ralph Linton's essay "100% American," which can be read online.)

In terms of biological inheritance, about 82 percent of the population is Caucasian (white), 12 percent is Negroid (black), 4 percent is Mongoloid (East Asian), and about 2 percent is indigenous (Amerindian, Alaskan, or Hawaiian) or of some other ancestry. Many Americans, of course, are of mixed ancestry or ethnicity. The foregoing figures can be confusing unless their meaning is understood. No link exists between race and culture. "White," for example, includes Hispanics, who can be completely integrated culturally or have strong Mexican, Cuban, Puerto Rican, or other Latin American cultural characteristics. An "Asian" can be from China, India, Indonesia, or some other area of the continent. Such "badges" of identity are all but meaningless. Throughout the country's history, most people—regardless of biological or cultural heritage—have willingly and enthusiastically become integrated into the American cultural "melting pot."

According to the 2000 U.S. Census, the U.S. population is descended from immigrants who trace their heritage to the following locations:

Germany	19.2 percent
Latin America	12.5 percent
Africa	12.1 percent
Ireland	10.8 percent
England	7.7 percent
Italy	5.6 percent
Asia	4.2 percent
Scandinavia	3.7 percent
Poland	3.2 percent
Other or unknown	21.0 percent

Hispanics are the most rapidly growing segment of the population, having surpassed African Americans in number during the late 1990s. If the trend of recent decades continues, by 2050, people of north European ancestry will no longer be the majority population. "Anglos" already are a minority in California, New Mexico, Texas, and Hawaii. Five other states—Arizona, Georgia, Maryland, Mississippi, and New York—are close behind: More than 40 percent of their populations are something other than north European in ancestral origin.

LANGUAGE

Language provides the "glue" that bonds a people together as a culture and society. Historically, Americans were a diverse people. They represented various cultures and spoke a variety of tongues. Through time, however, such differences largely vanished: People of all backgrounds joined together to form a uniquely American culture. Most Americans adopted English as their language through the process of *hierarchical diffusion*. Early settlement along the eastern seaboard was economically, socially, and politically dominated by the British. As a result, if

Hispanics are the fastest-growing segment of the U.S. population, particularly in such southern states as North Carolina, which experienced a 400 percent increase in its Hispanic population between 1990 and 2000. Here, Hispanics in Hickory, North Carolina, protest proposed immigration laws in 2006.

one was to succeed, he or she found it advantageous to adopt "British ways," including the English language. Nonetheless, American "English" itself has been patched together with words from many other tongues. How many words can you think of that are derived from Spanish? French? German?

Today, about 82 percent of Americans speak English as their primary tongue. Nearly 11 percent of the population, however, speaks Spanish as their first language, and that percentage is growing rapidly. About 4 percent of all Americans speak some other European tongue, and a small number, about 3 percent, speak an Asian, Pacific Island, Native American, or another language. The growing number of non-English-speaking people in the country poses a critical challenge to political leaders. Among countries that are linguistically divided, only tiny

Switzerland has a tradition of stability. Today, in numerous countries throughout the world, ethnic (including linguistic) diversity is a source of conflict. It was the primary factor that underlay the disintegration of both the Soviet Union and the former Yugoslavia. Diversity can contribute to social marginalization, economic deprivation, political powerlessness, cultural stratification, and a host of other problems. The United States must find a way to allow people to retain many elements of their culture while integrating those people into the nation's socioeconomic mainstream. Communicating through a common tongue is the easiest way for this objective to be achieved.

In traveling throughout the United States, one cannot help but recognize regional variations in language. These are evident in slang phrases, pronunciation, and words used in reference to particular things. Such language variations are called *dialects*. The South, for example, is known for its regional characteristic speech pattern popularly called the "Southern drawl." New Englanders are recognized by their clipped accents. The Midwestern dialect is the nation's "standard"; hence, it is the accent most widely used in national media.

A LAND OF MANY FAITHS

Perhaps more than any other people, Americans have a long history of religious tolerance. Many early immigrants came to the New World to escape religious persecution. This open-mindedness toward different faiths is evident in the tremendous diversity of faiths—nearly 3,000 organized religions!—practiced in the country today. About half of all Americans (52 percent) are Protestants; the leading denominations (in order of membership) are Baptist, Methodist, Lutheran, and Presbyterian. About one-fourth (24 percent) of the population is Roman Catholic. Because Hispanics are predominantly Roman Catholic, this number is growing. Other faiths include Latter Day Saints (Mormons), 2 percent; Jewish, 1 percent; Muslim, 1 percent; and other, 10 percent. About 10 percent of the population claims no religious faith. This figure is significant in that, in many European countries, up to half of the population is secular (nonreligious).

Most of the United States is "mixed" in terms of religious following. There are, however, some sections of the country that are dominated by a particular faith. The Southeast, for example, is overwhelmingly Baptist, whereas the upper Midwest is primarily Lutheran. Much of New England, southern Louisiana, and the Southwest are dominated by Roman Catholicism. Utah and southern Idaho are overwhelmingly Latter Day Saint (Mormon). The imprint of religion on the landscape is widespread. Churches, cemeteries, camps, and parochial schools and colleges are the most visible elements, but there are many others. Roadside crosses and shrines, and signs and other symbols that profess a faith, are commonplace in many parts of the country. Less obvious but of perhaps even greater significance is the impact of religion on laws. Restrictions are imposed on liquor and tobacco sales and Sunday "blue laws" (enforced closing), for example. Voting patterns on a host of political issues, such as abortion and stem-cell research, reflect religious beliefs.

FOODWAYS

Most of the world has a fairly standard diet (think "Chinese," "Mexican," "Italian," or some other ethnic food). What a people eat, the basic ingredients of their diet, how food is prepared, and how it is consumed remain basically unchanged through time. In contrast, Americans—at least those who love to eat diverse foods—are extremely fortunate. Every major cuisine in the world has contributed to the American diet. The closest city to the author's home is Sioux Falls, South Dakota—a community of about 150,000 people. Even in a city this size, one can choose from restaurants that represent more than a dozen different ethnicities. There are, of course, a number of Mexican, Italian, and Chinese restaurants, but there are others that specialize in Japanese, Middle Eastern, African, and Brazilian cuisine. The city's growing variety of dining options is further enhanced by restaurants that feature Indian, Thai, Continental (various European), Greek, and Irish menus.

The United States—as one might assume about a country comparable in area to Europe—also features a number of regional foodways. Many coastal areas specialize in seafood that ranges from Maine lobster to Louisiana Cajun, and various West Coast marine seafood preparations. Barbeque is a regional specialty in many areas from North Carolina to Texas and from Memphis to Kansas City; however, the person who expects a rack of ribs slathered in a tomato-based barbeque sauce certainly is in for a surprise when ordering barbeque in North Carolina. There, the delicacy is pork basted with vinegar and ground hot red pepper. The heartland foods tend to feature the basics: meat, potatoes, side dishes, and desserts. The Southwest is famous for its "Tex-Mex" variety of Mexican food and a cuisine that features regional ingredients.

Regional food terms also vary greatly. What would you call a long sandwich made with a variety of items? Your answer will serve as a badge of regional identity. The sandwiches are variously called grinders, heroes, hoagies, Italians, poor boys (or po' boys), submarines (or subs), and torpedoes in different regions. Spices and their use also vary greatly from region to region. From Louisiana (famous for its Tabasco sauce) westward to California, hot spices are commonplace, whereas in the nation's midsection food tends to be rather bland. Regional patterns also exist in such things as dips for french fries (ketchup, mayonnaise, or vinegar), what is put on cottage cheese (pepper or sugar), and condiments added to hot dogs and hamburgers (many regional variations).

Worldwide, most cultures are quite rigid in regard to beverage consumption. Some people drink tea (hot or iced, with or without lemon, sweet or unsweetened), whereas others drink only coffee. There are beer drinkers and wine drinkers (with meals). Among the latter, regional preferences exist in the type of wine(s) consumed. Germans, for example, prefer sweet wines, whereas the French prefer their wine "dry." In the United States, people are free to choose from any of these or many other options. One of the great joys of traveling within the United States is the opportunity to experience different regional foodways.

VARIED REGIONAL LANDSCAPES

America presents a fascinating mosaic of regional landscapes. The "look of the land," as geographer John Fraser Hart referred to landscape features and patterns, varies greatly throughout the country. Physical features—terrain, natural vegetation, and water features, in particular—differ greatly from region to region, as do systems of land division and patterns of rural settlement. The diversity of regional house and barn types, agricultural crops and field patterns, and how people make a living is astonishing as one travels around the country. This final section of the chapter is a brief tour of America's major regions. As you travel, try to identify major differences in the "look of the land" that make each region unique.

The Eastern Core

A core region is defined by its historical, economic, and demographic importance. These factors have helped contribute to a very strong sense of regional identity and pride. Here, in a belt that extends from New England to Chesapeake Bay, is where the United States took root. Here, the first quaint villages, fishing communities, farms, and logging camps were settled. Soon, manufacturing industries sprouted, and around them grew the nation's first manufacturing centers. Boston, New York, and Philadelphia eventually boomed to become world-class centers of industry, commerce, and services. Today, despite considerable out-migration during recent decades, this region continues to be the country's industrial, service, financial, and population core.

The Eastern Core possessed little in the way of natural resources. There were two resources, however, that people could put to use: Hundreds of water-powered lumber, textile, and flour mills and other industries sprung up around the region's many falls and rapids, and port cities grew around the region's several excellent natural harbors. With ample waterpower, abundant Appalachian coal, a large and eager immigrant workforce, and splendid seaports, a manufacturing economy sprouted and flourished. Several conditions were missing, though: raw materials and natural resources to process and large markets to which products could be sold. Here, of course, is where the major East Coast port cities played an important role. Industrial raw materials and natural resources could easily be imported, and manufactured goods could just as easily be exported. With this arrangement, it is little wonder that New York City ultimately became the world's leading economic center.

Today, this region still is the country's economic heartland, although it has experienced many problems. During the past half century, small farms have been abandoned and many old factories have closed. Hundreds of communities have experienced economic stagnation, population decline, and urban decay. There has been a substantial out-migration of both people and corporations. Fortunately, some portions of the Rust Belt are experiencing a revival. Many small communities, for example, are growing. People who have grown tired of living in the city are attracted to them because of their slower pace and a more pleasant rural environment. As the region has moved from primary and secondary to tertiary economic activities, they no longer need farm or factory jobs from which people can earn a living. Tourism and other services have replaced manufacturing in most communities.

Suburbs also are booming as they attract postindustrial businesses, including corporate headquarters, a variety of services, and information-based industries. Today, large malls, giant supermarkets and other retail stores, motels, gas stations, automobile dealers, and other corporate enterprises attest to an economic revival. They have replaced nearly all of the small family-owned and -operated businesses that thrived prior to the mid-twentieth century.

The Booming South

From Virginia southward to Florida and westward to Louisiana, an early slave-based economy thrived along the coastal plain. A century later, the upland South—Appalachia and the Cumberland Plateau, the Ozarks, and associated lowland plains and river valleys—began to fill in. Those who continue to hold an "Old South" stereotype are in for a shock when they first visit the region today. In the past half century, no section of the United States has experienced greater or more positive changes than has the South.

What once was the nation's most economically depressed region has been transformed into one of fast-paced social, political, and economic progress. An economy once dominated by agriculture is now based on growing intellectual capital, world-class research centers, new industries, expanded services, and thriving tourism. Atlanta, Georgia, is one of the country's fastest-growing metropolitan centers and the South's largest city. Hartsfield-Jackson Atlanta International Airport is now the world's busiest by a rather wide margin. With Disney World and many other attractions, the Orlando, Florida, area has become one of the world's primary tourist destinations. The future for the South is extremely bright.

The Farm- and Factory-Dominated Midwest

Sandwiched between the Great Lakes, the Appalachian Mountains, and the Missouri River, the Midwest is the nation's "breadbasket" and historical industrial heartland. This region generally coincides with the Corn Belt, one of the world's leading agricultural regions. Because of the booming ethanol industry, the price of corn has nearly doubled in the period of

Since it opened in 1971, the Walt Disney World Resort has made the Orlando, Florida, area a popular tourist destination. Here, Mickey Mouse and his fellow Disney characters gather outside Cinderella Castle shortly before the resort's grand opening.

2005–2007, and it shows no sign of declining. This is a good sign for the region's farmers.

The Midwest also was the country's industrial core. Many of its cities became famous for a particular product that they produced. (How many professional athletic team names reflect their city's economic importance? For example, with what communities do you associate the Brewers, Pistons, Steelers, and Packers?) Detroit was once the center of the automobile industry, which depended on tires from Akron, Ohio, and steel from Pittsburgh, Pennsylvania. Chicago grew as the nation's transportation hub—a center for rail, highway, air, and even water transportation. With its strong German ethnic heritage, Milwaukee became widely known for its beer production. St. Louis, a regional industrial center and important Mississippi River port city, is proud of its heritage as the "Gateway to the West." In many respects, the "heartland," as it often is called, continues to mirror the traditions and values on which the country was based.

The Spacious Interior West

The interior West occupies slightly more than half of the coterminous United States. It extends from Texas northward to the Dakotas and westward to the Sierra Nevada and Cascades. The Great Plains, the Rocky Mountains, and the interior basins and plateaus are the region's major physiographic provinces. The region features an environment that can be quite challenging. From south to north, extreme summer heat gives way to frigid winter cold. From east to west, precipitation decreases and severe drought is a frequent occurrence. Throughout much of the region, population densities are quite low, often fewer than two people per square mile (one per square kilometer). The Great Plains in particular is a region of out-migration, resulting in hundreds of struggling rural communities. Small farms and ranches have given way to huge operations that are measured in square miles rather than in acres.

Ethnically, the region is one of considerable diversity. It contains the nation's highest population of Native Americans. In the

Southwest, a strong Hispanic cultural heritage has centuries-old roots. While in the northern Great Plains, Germans, Russians (many of whom trace their ancestry to Germans from Russia), and Norwegians were the major groups that flocked to that region. Their landscape imprint often is visible in their settlements, agricultural practices, and place names.

Economically, several regional patterns can be identified. Agricultural crops are important in the wetter eastern margin. Grains, soybeans, and hay are dominant in the north, and cotton is a major crop in the south. Moving westward, conditions become drier and agricultural activity changes to livestock ranching and mixed irrigated and dry-land farming.

In the Mountain West, mineral extraction, logging, scattered pockets of agriculture, and tourism prevail. Initially, gold and silver mining drew many prospectors in search of easy wealth. The western mountains are dotted with old mining centers, many of which became ghost towns when the ore played out. South Dakota's Black Hills produced more gold than any other location in the world. Much of the activity was centered around the towns of Lead (pronounced *leed*) and Deadwood. Today, all of the area's mines are closed, but as has happened to many other former mining towns, the communities are once again thriving. Deadwood has become a major tourist center that offers casino gambling, mountain landscapes, nearby ski resorts, and other tourist attractions—including a rich history that includes "Calamity" Jane and "Wild Bill" Hickok.

Much of the West prospered from copper mining. Butte, Montana—site of the famous Berkeley Pit—was once the largest city in the United States between St. Louis and San Francisco. Many other communities in Arizona, New Mexico, and Utah thrived as copper mining centers. In Texas and Oklahoma, rich oil deposits fueled widespread economic development. Today, coal fields, oil and natural gas deposits, and uranium support economic growth in many areas of the West.

Paradoxically, the western interior is the region of greatest out-migration and also the greatest population gain. Growth

According to the 2000 U.S. Census, Las Vegas, Nevada, was the fastest-growing city in the United States. During the 1990s, its population increased by more than 83 percent. Here, a billboard announces the construction of a new housing development outside Las Vegas in 2007.

has been particularly explosive in the Southwest, a portion of the Sun Belt that extends from Texas westward to Arizona and Nevada. Recently, Las Vegas and Nevada surpassed Phoenix and Arizona as the country's fastest-growing city and state, respectively. The desert oasis gambling and entertainment center has become one of the world's leading tourist destinations. Cities such as San Antonio, Houston, Dallas, Albuquerque, San Antonio, and Denver also have grown rapidly during recent decades.

The Diverse Pacific Realm

No part of the United States can match the Pacific Coast region (including Alaska and Hawaii) in terms of diversity. In Chapter 2, you learned of the region's spectacular natural landscapes and environmental extremes. The region also offers the country's greatest ethnic diversity. Nowhere is this more evident than in Anchorage, Alaska. Anchorage School District students represent families that speak more than 100 different native languages! In California, people of north European descent became a minority early in the twenty-first century. They have been replaced primarily by Latin Americans and Asians.

Excluding California's Central Valley—the nation's most productive agricultural area—the Pacific Realm is dominated by cities. More than 30 million people live in the nearly continuous urban area that extends from San Diego to metropolitan Los Angeles and northward to San Francisco. For decades, California has been the nation's leader in population, agricultural production, manufacturing, trade and commerce, and services, including tourism. It has also been the world's foremost center of commercial popular culture. The media industry—Hollywood's motion pictures, various genres of music, radio and television, and the print media—in particular, has had a huge impact on popular culture fads and trends worldwide.

Remarkable diversity also is evident in the region's agriculture. Most agricultural regions specialize in a particular crop—hence, the regional recognition of corn, wheat, cotton, and dairy "belts." In California, Oregon, and Washington, however, individual counties may produce more than 70 agricultural crops! Still, some small areas in the region have become recognized for a single crop. The Napa and Sonoma valleys are famous for their vineyards and world-class wines, just as Washington's Yakima Valley is well known for its apples and other fruits. Gilroy, California, is the nation's self-proclaimed "Garlic Capital," a role that nearby communities Castroville and Watsonville claim for artichokes and strawberries, respectively.

The United States is as dynamic as it is diverse. Much like a kaleidoscope, it will continue to undergo changes, some anticipated and others perhaps unexpected. A half century ago, few people, for example, could have forecasted the explosive population and economic growth that has occurred through-out the South and Southwest during recent decades. This is particularly true of the nation's hottest and driest, yet fastest-growing, spots: Arizona and Nevada. The same can be said for the incredible changes that have occurred in the South since the 1960s. An area once stereotyped as being bigoted and impoverished is today a model of social stability and economic prosperity. Throughout its history, the United States has constantly adjusted to changing conditions and grasped new opportunities. One thing is certain in regard to life in the United States: It will change and Americans will adapt and thrive.

CHAPTER

8

The United States Looks Ahead

*N*ow is but a minute blip on the span of time. It is the product of countless past processes and events. By looking to the past, we can better understand the present, and the past also provides keys to predicting the future. This chapter attempts to answer a very difficult question: What does the future hold for the United States of America? Will the country continue to be a prosperous and powerful beacon of hope within an increasingly troubled and fragmented world? Or, as has happened to all previous powers, will the United States gradually wither away to become little more than another past civilization in the dustbin of historical geography? Pessimists believe that dusk is settling on America's "moment in the sun." Optimists, however, see a bright future for the country and its more than 300 million people. Who is right? Perhaps there is at least some support for both positions. Let us closely examine the evidence and attempt to determine what it may foretell.

During the author's lifetime, great changes have occurred within the natural environment. Many vital mineral resources have dwindled in both quantity and quality. Some natural elements, including woodlands, soils, water, fauna, and even the air we breathe became seriously threatened. Science and technology, however, actually allowed our resource base to expand. At the same time, the country has been able to import many of the resources (such as petroleum) in which it is now deficient. Only an affluent society can afford the costly luxury of maintaining a clean, safe, and sustainable environment. The United States has spent some $2 trillion to mitigate or reverse pollution and other forms of environmental damage. The result is that, today, much of the country's water and air are cleaner and there is more forested area and abundant wildlife than existed a half century ago. New forms of energy, including biofuels and wind, solar, and geothermal power, are being developed. The increased use of nuclear energy holds great promise if safety of production and waste disposal can be ensured.

Environmental hazards surely will become more severe as fires, storms, floods, earth flows and slides, earthquakes, and tsunamis take an ever-increasing toll on life and property. It is doubtful that nature's fury will increase. Rather, as the population continues to grow, people and property will become increasingly vulnerable to nature's wrath. They will continue to be drawn to hazard-prone amenity areas such as coastal zones, forested areas, volcanic mountains, and geologic faults. One environmental change remains a question mark—the possible impact of warming temperatures. In this context, let us simply accept the fact that data strongly point to a warming Earth and not become entangled in the rancorous debate over its cause. If temperatures continue to warm, several things are certain: Alaska will become much warmer, as will much of the remainder of the United States; the sea level will rise, placing coastal cities and other developments in severe jeopardy (as already has occurred in below-sea level New Orleans); summer tropical storms may increase in number and intensity; some parts of the country will become drier while

Over the last couple of decades, the fertility rate has continued to drop in the United States and is now below the replacement rate of 2.1 children per woman. The United States will have to continue to welcome immigrants if it hopes to match its declining fertility rate. Here, a diverse group of kindergartners in Los Angeles's Lycee International School work together on a project.

others receive increased moisture; and ecosystems will change in response to changing temperature and moisture conditions. If you enjoy snow skiing, you had better enjoy it now!

Population, settlement, and culture all will experience considerable change in the decades ahead. Fertility should continue to drop from its current rate that is now below the replacement level of 2.1. Because of migration, however, the country's population continues to increase at a rate of about 0.9 percent each year. Whether this rate of in-migration (year-in, year-out, the world's highest) will continue is the subject of heated debate with demographic, cultural, social, economic, and political implications.

One thing is certain: The country's population is aging. As the workforce grows older and eventually retires, an increasing number of young workers will be needed. Where will they come from? Already, millions of international workers are in the country, an estimated 11 to 13 million of them undocumented (illegal). Were they to leave, the country's economy would crumble. This issue begs bipartisan political attention and a resolution that is fair to all parties involved. It can be stated with considerable certainty that racial, cultural, and ethnic diversity will continue to expand as a result of continued in-migration and higher fertility rates among migrants. Both the Anglo-European and the immigrant population will have to adapt to these changes. Of greatest importance is the issue of cultural assimilation. By becoming "American," people—regardless of their heritage—are much better able to participate in and benefit from the country's social, economic, and political opportunities.

Settlement patterns—where people live—have changed greatly during the past 50 years, a trend that certainly will continue in the foreseeable future. The average American moves 11 times, a number that may increase in the coming decades as the population becomes even more mobile. Throughout history, most people have moved in search of economic gain. Today, the reasons are changing. For some time now, the United States has been undergoing the transition from an industrial economy to one based on the provision of services. People today are much less tied to factory and service jobs in industrial cities. Many people now hold jobs that are much less place specific—that is, they can live wherever they choose and continue to work at their jobs. Millions of retirees, too, are now relatively free to choose a location that suits their income, desires, and needs. A combination of these two factors has resulted in a massive change in where people have settled during the past 50 years. Generally, there has been a huge migration from cold to warm climates and from congested urban centers to suburbs and amenity areas—coasts, mountains, lakeshores, and other attractive locations. For the foreseeable future, at least, this trend no doubt will continue. It will result in a much different map of population distribution.

In regard to government, it may seem that nearly everyone is displeased with the way the U.S. political system is working. Most people are tired of costly mudslinging campaigns, the heavy-handed influence of lobbyists, "pork-barrel" politics, leaders who place politics before country, and outright corruption. These conditions contribute to a loss of confidence in the government and result in a political system that often falls far short of successfully addressing national, and international issues, interests, concerns, and needs. Onetime British Prime Minister Winston Churchill reportedly observed that "democracy is the worst form of government except all those other forms that have been tried from time to time." The wisdom contained in his comment certainly holds true for the U.S. government. Some adjustments can and should be made in the way in which the nation's political affairs and future well-being are being handled. With all of its blemishes, however, the Constitution and the political system it created have stood the test of time. The American brand of constitutional democracy should continue to serve the country well in the future.

America's economy is the world's strongest, having produced nearly $13 trillion in goods and services during 2006. For decades, the primary threat to the country's economic supremacy appeared to be from Japan. Today, however, the challenge comes from China ($10 trillion), rather than from Japan ($4.5 trillion). Spend a few moments looking around your home—how many items can you find with a "Made in China" label? Americans have turned to China for countless manufactured goods simply because they can be produced at a much lower cost in a developing country with the world's largest labor pool.

Economically, the United States does, indeed, face a number of challenges, changes, and opportunities. Increasingly, the country must turn to foreign sources for energy that is essential to economic growth. To reduce this dependence, bold steps must be taken to ensure energy self-sufficiency. Many of the alternative energy sources (such as wind and ethanol) also will reduce or eliminate atmospheric and other forms of pollution.

Until self-sufficiency is achieved, it is essential that the country maintain stable access to foreign sources such as the Middle East, Mexico, Nigeria, and Venezuela.

This country also is increasingly dependent on foreign sources for workers. This is true for blue-collar, low-wage laborers and also highly skilled white-collar workers. In many respects, the U.S. educational system has failed to adequately prepare young people to compete in a postindustrial, information-age, global economy. The country is unable to meet its demand for highly skilled scientists, engineers, technicians, physicians, and others, yet these highly educated workers are desperately needed to provide the brainpower on which economic growth and development depend. In addition, test after test has shown that America's young are woefully ignorant of the world they are about to inherit. It is imperative that geography be (re)introduced into the curriculum.

Other dynamics are at work changing the face of the U.S. economy. The country has undergone a transition from primarily small, family-owned and -operated businesses to huge corporations. Gone are the "mom and pop" motels, restaurants, grocery and drug stores, and service stations that once dotted the landscape. They have been replaced by huge, often multinational, impersonal, chain retail and service outlets. There are signs of change, however: Throughout the country, specialty shops and services are increasing in number and variety.

Perhaps no industry better illustrates these changes than does beer brewing. During the first half of the twentieth century, nearly every community had its own brewery. Thousands of brands were available, most of them sold within a small marketing area, often only within the community itself. Several decades ago, however, nearly all of these small breweries were gone. Most of the nation's beer was manufactured by a handful of huge companies. This resulted in the same few brands being marketed throughout most, if not all, of the country. Today, however, hundreds of microbreweries and brand labels once

Unfortunately for the American public, the "mom and pop" stores of yesteryear have been replaced by megastores such as Wal-Mart, the world's largest retailer. Although the Arkansas-based company offers discounted goods, it has recently come under fire for carrying mostly foreign-made products.

again offer a huge variety of beers. The future appears to hold an ever-increasing number of options.

Further consolidation, fueled by the "cult of bigness," certainly will continue. The economy of scale will benefit consumers by offering lower prices but may also offer fewer choices. At the other extreme, specialty shops of all kinds will make available an ever-increasing variety of high-quality products and services, although at a higher cost.

Finally, what does the future hold for regional changes? Looking back through time, changes have occurred at a blurring pace. California's population and economy boomed to become the nation's most populated state and the fifth-richest political unit on Earth. With water control and diversion and the advent of air-conditioning, the once sleepy, dusty, parched desert

Southwest boomed. For a variety of reasons, the once very traditional, relatively poor, and socially restrictive South blossomed as well. With migration to the Sun Belt, however, what once was the nation's economic heartland dwindled in importance to become the Snow Belt or Rust Belt. Today, the South, Southwest, and Mountain and Pacific West are the multiple engines of the country's demographic and economic growth, and what once was the nation's population and economic heartland—the interior plains and lowlands and the industrial Northeast—are now regions of out-migration and waning economic importance.

Fifty years ago, coastal zones and remote mountainous and hilly areas (such as the Mountain West and "hillbilly" country of the Ozarks and Appalachians) supported very few people. Today, these areas are experiencing explosive population and economic growth. The next half century will bring many additional regional shifts. Changes in social and economic conditions, real estate prices, urban environments, and a host of other factors will serve as push-and-pull factors that alter the settlement landscape and character.

Cultural geographer and urban planner Kyle Ezell foresees several major changes in settlement. What he called "Escape Lands" will become increasingly attractive as people seek a more comfortable, less stressful, slower-paced life; that is, a rural or small-town life. Ezell also foresees rebirth of the inner city as redevelopment projects vastly improve midcity living conditions. In regard to population shift, the author (a South Dakotan by choice) will go out on a limb and make a prediction. Despite their often harsh weather and seemingly bleak and endless terrain, within the next few decades, much of the Midwest and Great Plains will be (re)discovered and experience a "boom"!

In conclusion, the future of the United States of America rests in the hands of the generation of young people for whom books in this series are designed. I am optimistic that your generation will serve your country well, thereby ensuring not only its future prosperity, but securing your own destiny as well.

Facts at a Glance

Physical Geography

Location North America (continent); Northern America (culture realm); bordering the North Atlantic Ocean and the North Pacific Ocean; between Canada and Mexico

Area 3,718,712 square miles (9,826,630 square kilometers), ranking third among the world's countries in area; *land:* 3,537,438 square miles (9,161,923 square kilometers); *water:* 256,645 square miles (664,707 square kilometers); includes 50 states and the District of Columbia; extends from approximately 19°N in Hawaii to 71°N in Alaska and 67°W in Maine to 173°E in Alaska's Aleutian Islands

Boundaries 7,478 miles (12,034 kilometers) of land border— 5,526 miles (8,893 kilometers) with Canada and 1,952 miles (3,141 kilometers) with Mexico; 12,380 miles (19,924 kilometers) of coastline

Climate Mostly temperate, with tropical conditions in Hawaii and southern Florida, arctic in Alaska, and semiarid to arid in much of the interior West and the Southwest; only country in the world to have 11 of the world's climates and ecosystems within its territory; great extremes of temperature and precipitation from region to region; subject to all weather-related storms, including tornadoes and hurricanes

Terrain Eastern coastal plain backed by Appalachian Mountains; vast interior lowland plains; high mountains, basin and range topography, large plateaus in the west; rugged mountains and broad river valleys in Alaska; volcanic mountains and other features in Hawaii

Elevation Extremes Lowest point is Death Valley, California, 282 feet (86 meters) below sea level; highest point is Denali (Mount McKinley), Alaska, 20,320 feet (6,194 meters)

Land Use Other, 82%; arable land, 18%; permanent crops, 0.21%

Irrigated Land 86,428 square miles (223,850 square kilometers), an area roughly the size of Utah

Natural Hazards Earthquakes, volcanic eruptions, tsunamis, and earth slides in the West; tornadoes in the Midwest and Southeast; hurricanes along the Atlantic and Gulf

127

coasts; forest fires and flooding in many areas; perma-
frost in Alaska

Natural Resources Mineral fuels (coal, petroleum, natural gas, uranium);
numerous metals and construction materials; abundant
soil, forest, and fauna resources

Environmental Issues Widespread air and water pollution; the United States
is the world's largest emitter of carbon dioxide from
the burning of fossil fuels; problems related to runoff of
pesticides, herbicides, and fertilizers; limited freshwater
resources throughout much of the West; desertification;
declining marine resources

People

Population 301,139,947 (July 2007 est.); males, 148,006,279 (July 2007
est.); females, 153,133,668 (March 2007 est.)

Population Density 80 per square mile (30 per square kilometer)

Population Growth Rate 0.89% (2007 est.)

Net Migration Rate 3.05 migrant(s)/1,000 population (2007 est.)

Fertility Rate 2.09 children born per woman (2.1 is the
replacement rate)

Birthrate 14 per 1,000 population (2007 est.)

Death Rate 8 per 1,000 population (2007 est.)

Life Expectancy at Birth Total population: 78 years (male, 75 years; female,
81 years)

Median Age 36.6 years; male, 35.3 years; female, 37.9 years (2007 est.)

Ethnic Groups Caucasian (European), 81.7%; Negroid (African), 12.9%;
Mongoloid (Asian), 3.8%

Religion Protestant, 52%; Roman Catholic, 24%; Mormon, 2%;
Jewish, 1%; Muslim, 1%; other, 10%; none, 10%

Languages English, 82.1%; Spanish, 10.7%; other European, 3.8%;
Pacific island, 2.7%; other, 0.7%

Literacy (Age 15 and over can read and write) Total population:
99% (male, 99.0%; female, 99.0%) (2003 est.)

Economy

Currency U.S. dollar (USD)

GDP Purchasing Power
Parity (PPP) $13.13 trillion (2006 est.)

GDP Per Capita $43,500 (2006 estimate)

128

Labor Force	151.4 million (includes unemployed) (2006 est.)
Unemployment	4.8% (October 2006 est.)
Labor Force by Occupation	Managerial, professional, and technical, 34.9%; sales and office, 25%; manufacturing, extraction, transportation, and crafts, 22.9%; other services, 16.5%; farming, forestry, and fishing, 0.7%
Agricultural Products	Wheat, corn, other grains, fruits, vegetables, cotton; beef, pork, poultry, dairy products; fish; forest products
Industries	Leading industrial power in the world, highly diversified and technologically advanced; petroleum, steel, motor vehicles, aerospace, telecommunications, chemicals, electronics, food processing, consumer goods, lumber, mining
Exports	$1.024 trillion f.o.b. (2006 estimate)
Export Commodities	Capital goods, 49% (transistors, aircraft, motor vehicle parts, computers, telecommunications equipment); industrial supplies, 26.8%; consumer goods, 15% (automobiles, medicines); agricultural products, 4.9% (soybeans, fruit, corn)
Imports	$1.869 trillion f.o.b. (2006 estimate)
Import Commodities	Industrial supplies, 32.9% (crude oil); consumer goods, 31.8% (automobiles, clothing, medicines, furniture, toys); capital goods, 30.4% (computers, telecommunications equipment, motor vehicle parts, office machines, electric power machinery); agricultural products, 4.9%
Leading Trade Partners	Exports: Canada, 23.4%; Mexico, 13.3%; Japan, 6.1%; China, 4.6%; U.K., 4.3%; Imports: Canada, 16.9%; China, 15%; Mexico, 10%; Japan, 8.2%; Germany, 5%
Transportation	Roadways: 3,995,644 miles (6,430,366 kilometers), of which 2,588,079 miles (4,165,110 kilometers) are paved, including 46,608 miles (75,009 kilometers) of expressways; Railways: 140,806 miles (226,605 kilometers); Airports: 9,739–5,119 are paved runways; Waterways: 25,482 miles (41,009 kilometers); 12,000 miles (19,312 kilometers) used for commerce

Government

Country Name	Conventional long form: United States of America; conventional short form: United States; America; abbreviated form: U.S.A., U.S.
Capital City	Washington, D.C. (District of Columbia)
Type of Government	Constitution-based federal republic with strong tradition of democracy
Head of Government	President George W. Bush (since January 20, 2001)
Independence	July 4, 1776 (from Great Britain)
Administrative Divisions	50 states, one district (D.C.), numerous dependent areas
Constitution	September 17, 1787 (effective March 4, 1789)
Branches of Government	Executive (president); legislative (bicameral, with 435-seat House of Representatives and 100-seat Senate); judicial (Supreme Court, with nine appointed justices; U.S. Courts of Appeal; U.S. District Courts; state and county courts

Communications

TV Stations	2,218; (219 million television sets)
Radio Stations	13,750 (8,961 FM, 4,789 AM); (575 million radios)
Phones	(Line) 268 million; (cell) 219 million
Internet Users	205 million (2005)
Internet Service Providers	7,000

* Source: *CIA-The World Factbook* (2007)

B.C.

<20000 Possible human presence in the United States.

<12000 Ice age glaciers begin to recede.

circa 10000 Most of United States inhabited by native peoples.

A.D.

1497 John Cabot is the first documented European explorer to reach the shores of Northern America and possibly New England.

1507 The name "America" first appears on a map.

1540 Francisco Coronado leads a band of Spanish explorers into present-day New Mexico and beyond.

1565 Spaniards establish St. Augustine (Florida), which becomes the first permanent settled European community in Northern America.

1607 British settle at Jamestown (Virginia).

1610 Spanish settle Santa Fe (New Mexico).

1776 American Revolution begins; America declares independence on July 4.

1803 United States buys the Louisiana Territory from France for $15 million, expanding its landholdings by 800,000 square miles (2 million square kilometers).

1804–1806 President Thomas Jefferson sends the Corps of Discovery, an expedition headed by Merriwether Lewis and William Clark, to explore the west to the shores of the Pacific Ocean.

1848 Gold is discovered at Sutter's Mill, east of San Francisco, California, resulting in the massive gold rush of 1849.

1861–1865 Civil War bitterly divides the United States, pitting the slaveholding Southern states against the North.

1863 President Abraham Lincoln's leadership leads to the Emancipation Proclamation, which frees slaves in the United States.

1867 Alaska is purchased from Russia for $7.2 million.

1869 United States completes the first transcontinental railway.

1900 Galveston (Texas) hurricane kills as many as 8,000 people in Northern America's greatest natural disaster as measured by loss of life.

1906	San Francisco earthquake kills 500 people and nearly destroys the city.
1929	Great Depression begins, bringing financial ruin to millions.
1930s	Much of interior Northern America suffers severe drought that results in "dust bowl" conditions; thousands of displaced people migrate to California, beginning the state's population boom.
1941–1945	United States is involved in World War II.
1959	Alaska and Hawaii, respectively, become the forty-ninth and fiftieth U.S. states, and the current flag is adopted.
1964	Alaska experiences a 9.2 magnitude earthquake, perhaps the strongest quake ever recorded, that results in more than 130 deaths.
1980	Mount St. Helens (Washington) erupts violently, killing 57 people and destroying an area of several thousand square miles.
1988	United States and Canada sign the Free Trade Agreement.
1992	Hurricane Andrew strikes Florida and Louisiana, resulting in a (then) record $25 billion in property losses.
1994	North American Free Trade Agreement (NAFTA) includes Mexico and spurs trade among the United States, Canada, and Mexico.
2001	On September 11, terrorists hijack four commercial flights and attack the Twin Towers of the World Trade Center in New York City and the Pentagon in Washington, D.C.; a fourth plane crashes in Pennsylvania. All told, an estimated 3,000 lives are lost.
2005	In August, Hurricane Katrina strikes the Louisiana and Mississippi Gulf Coast, killing nearly 2,000 people and inflicting more than $80 billion in damage.

Atlas of the United States of America. Washington, D.C. United States Department of the Interior—U. S. Geological Survey, 1970.

Garrett, Wilbur E., ed. *Atlas of North America.* Washington, D.C.: National Geographic Society, 1985.

——, ed. *Historical Atlas of the United States.* Washington, D.C.: National Geographic Society, 1988.

McKnight, Tom L. *Regional Geography of the United States and Canada.* Upper Saddle River, N.J.: Pearson Education, 4th edition, 2004.

Rooney, John F. Jr., Wilbur Zelinsky, and Dean R. Louder, eds. *This Remarkable Continent: An Atlas of United States and Canadian Society and Cultures.* College Station: Texas A&M University Press, 1982.

Further Reading

Atlas of the United States of America. Washington, D.C. United States Department of the Interior—U.S. Geological Survey, 1970.

Birdsall, Stephen S., John W. Florin, and Margo L. Price. *Regional Landscapes of the United States and Canada.* New York: John Wiley & Sons, 1999.

Boal, Frederick W., and Stephen A. Royle, eds. *North America: A Geographical Mosaic.* London: Arnold, 1999.

Garreau, Joel. *The Nine Nations of North America.* Boston: Houghton Mifflin Company, 1981.

Garrett, Wilbur E., ed. *Atlas of North America.* Washington, D.C.: National Geographic Society, 1985.

——, ed. *Historical Atlas of the United States.* Washington, D.C.: National Geographic Society, 1988.

Hakim, Joy. *The First Americans, Prehistory—1608.* New York: Oxford University Press, 2003.

Hart, John Fraser. *The Look of the Land.* Englewood Cliffs, N.J.: Prentice-Hall, 1975.

King, David C. *Smithsonian Children's Encyclopedia of American History.* New York: DK Publishing, 2003.

McKnight, Tom L. *Regional Geography of the United States and Canada,* fourth edition. Upper Saddle River, N.J.: Pearson Education, 2004.

McNeese, Tim. *The Mississippi River.* Philadelphia: Chelsea House, 2004.

Rooney, John F. Jr., Wilbur Zelinsky, and Dean R. Louder, eds. *This Remarkable Continent: An Atlas of United States and Canadian Society and Cultures.* College Station: Texas A&M University Press, 1982.

Web sites

CIA World Factbook

https://www.cia.gov/library/publications/the-world-factbook/geos/us.html

Facts on the United States

http://www.infoplease.com/states.html

The National Atlas of the United States

http://nationalatlas.gov/

Regions of the United States

http://usa.usembassy.de/travel-regions.htm

NOTE: For further and current information on the United States and any of its political subunits or specific topics such as the environment and population, economic, political, social, or other data, please use Internet search engines as appropriate. An excellent general information source for any of the world's countries is *www.cia.gov/cia/publications/factbook*; demographic data are available from a number of sources, including *http://members.aol.com/bowermanb/population.html* and *www.census.gov.*

Picture Credits

Index

Index

About the Author

CHARLES F. GRITZNER is distinguished professor of geography at South Dakota State University in Brookings. He is now in his fifth decade of college teaching, scholarly research, and writing. In addition to teaching, he enjoys traveling, writing, working with teachers, and sharing his love of geography with students and readers alike. As the series editor and a frequent author for the Chelsea House MODERN WORLD NATIONS and MODERN WORLD CULTURES series, as well as the author of the three-volume series GEOGRAPHY OF EXTREME ENVIRONMENTS, he has a wonderful opportunity to combine each of these "hobbies." Gritzner has traveled extensively in all 50 states (including having lived in seven).

Professionally, Gritzner has served as both president and executive director of the National Council for Geographic Education. He has received numerous national awards in recognition of his academic and teaching achievements, including the NCGE's George J. Miller Award for Distinguished Service to geography and geographic education and both the Distinguished Teaching Achievement Award and Gilbert M. Grosvenor Honors in Geography Education from the Association of American Geographers.